THE PAUL OF SURPRISES

THE PAUL OF SURPRISES

His Vision of the Christian Life

Geoffrey Turner

DARTON · LONGMAN + TODD

First published in Great Britain in 2012 by
Darton, Longman and Todd Ltd
1 Spencer Court
140 – 142 Wandsworth High Street
London
SW18 4JJ

ISBN: 978-0-232-52892-3

A catalogue record for this book is available from the British Library.

Phototypeset by Kerrypress Ltd, Luton, Bedfordshire.
Printed and bound by Scandbook AB

Contents

Acknowledgements

Quotations from the Bible are normally from the New Revised Standard Version, though I have occasionally made small emendations to bring out what I take to be the meaning of the Greek in the New Testament, especially in Chapter 5.

New Revised Standard Version Bible: Anglicized Edition, copyright 1989, 1995, Division of Christian Education of the National Council of the Churches of Christ in the United States of America. Used by permission. All rights reserved.

Some of the ideas in this book have appeared in a different form in the following articles:

'Spiritual Identification with Christ: Jon Sobrino, the CDF and St Paul' in *New Blackfriars*, September 2007, pp. 539–48;

'The Righteousness of God in Psalms and Romans' in *Scottish Journal of Theology*, July 2010, pp. 285–301;

'The Christian Life as Slavery: Paul's Subversive Metaphor' in *The Heythrop Journal*, forthcoming.

Introduction

Christianity is not popular in Britain or Europe generally at the moment and is often looked on with intellectual and sometimes even moral disdain. I have heard it said that people in the West have grown tired of Christianity and need a break from it. The church is certainly looking tired and there is evidence of many people wanting to expunge it from their cultural memory. Yet at the same time, swathes of people who turn away from the church, particularly younger people who have had no direct connection with it, are actually quite ignorant of what Christianity is about. They seem to be rejecting something they neither know nor understand. Sometimes secular objections present themselves as moral outrage at some of the teaching of the church or at its behaviour (with an accompanying suggestion of hypocrisy), and sometimes objections come as an intellectual dismissal of Christian beliefs which assumes that rationality is all on the side of secularism. When objections are based on an accurate understanding of Christianity one can hardly complain but all too often they come from ignorance or inadequate understanding. You can see that in the fruitless debates about atheism that involve Richard Dawkins or his supporters. Any authentic presentation of Christianity at the present time in the West, then, is bound to be counter-cultural, and this book is just that.

Much of the work that needs to be done to re-establish the respectability of Christianity will be about arguing the intellectual case for Christianity, but this will only touch a minority and it can be argued that Christianity is not primarily an intellectual affair – though it *is* that. It is more a practical business about how one lives

1

one's life. Choosing to be Christian means choosing a way of life, a pattern of behaviour which from day to day expresses one's beliefs and values and hopes. It is about life and about preparing for death – we are, as Heidegger said, beings oriented towards death. Christianity is not something bolted on to everyday life which you might put into operation on Sundays. It is not a hobby or a pastime for those with a taste for the religious, with all the campness that suggests. The Christian life is about how we do everything, it is all-pervasive. Some may find this pattern of life unappealing or even risible but others might be attracted to it as an alternative to the superficiality and self-indulgence of current secular values and behaviours. Christianity offers a grown-up morality and is far from being a crutch for the weak. Indeed when taken seriously it is demanding and not for the self-indulgent. It is also something that will never be fully achieved; the persistence of sin and the constraints of our social and political world will see to that.

That is what this book is about: the Christian life. It is also a study in St Paul. It focuses on Paul in order to keep the range of the material manageable and also because of the immense value of his particular contribution to our understanding of the Christian life. It hardly needs to be said that Paul came from a quite different culture from ours and some of what he says is limited by his time, but human experience has not changed that much over the centuries and most of what he wrote still offers an incisive and defining picture of what is involved in living as a Christian. Many may be surprised by what he has to say. He is far from being the arid theologian of some people's imagination.

This book covers some of Paul's ethics. The first chapter shows that his ethics is primarily about character, the kind of person you have to become, rather than about following rules or laws (which is how Christian morality sometimes presents itself, especially to the young). His is an ethics that flows into spirituality. Paul's vision of the Christian life is about individual moral and spiritual development and how it can be supported in social groups (i.e., churches, voluntary associations, but also schools and places of employment, though these can be inimical to the development of good character). This book is also about, or is at least underpinned by, an understanding of the theology of Paul and particularly his Christology. So we are engaged with an area where ethics and spirituality and theology come together and overlap in Paul.

There are a couple of preliminary issues that we should deal with at this point. First, the Jewishness of Paul. Historically this has often been ignored and Paul has been tipped on his head to be presented as the original Christian opponent of Judaism, and this even as early as the second century. Particularly influential is the way he has been used at a later time in the Lutheran tradition to support Martin Luther's antithesis between 'law' and 'gospel'. This is an antithesis that Luther and his followers have taken to stand for Judaism and Christianity, with the implication that they are of their nature in opposition. A more recent and rather different move has been to label Paul as 'the founder of Christianity', which seems to be an attempt to dissociate Jesus from Paul and the Christianity which came after him, so that Jesus can be presented as an unobjectionable and even admirable Jewish prophet and martyr – but not the intentional founder of a new religion that was to become antagonistic to Judaism. The doubtful privilege of founding Christianity then becomes Paul's. The fact of the matter is that we do not know all that much about Paul's influence on the early church in the years after his death. His influence seems to have faded quite quickly judging by 2 Peter, a letter that tells us that many in the church found Paul difficult to understand and distorted his meaning. His greatest influence in the second century seems to have been on Marcion who misunderstood him as much as anyone ever has. Paul *is* difficult and it explains why he came to be remembered less as a theologian and more as a missionary and martyr. Because of recent attempts to drive a wedge between Jesus and Paul, it is important to consider how far they have a common message, bearing in mind that Paul had to adapt that message to new circumstances.

Jews have certainly seen Paul as their enemy, and not entirely without justification when you take a line like 'Christ is the end of the law' out of context. However, context is everything. Paul was killed in the early 60s and if, as tradition says, this happened during Nero's persecution, his death would have been in AD 64 or 65, though it is possible that his trial and execution took place two or three years earlier. During the time Paul was writing his letters (they were all written in the 50s or at the beginning of the 60s) there was no independent religion that could have been identified as Christianity. There were just religious groups within Judaism. At the time of Paul's own conversion, all Christ-believers were Jewish. According to the New Testament, the first Gentiles to be baptised were Cornelius and his family in Acts 10, and Luke suggests that the name Christian was used for the first time shortly after that, though it is probably anachronistic to place it quite so early (Acts 11:26). Up to that time, probably the early or middle 40s, the Jesus movement was an entirely Jewish affair, if our sources are to be trusted. A little later, in AD 48, a council was held in Jerusalem, not to decide whether Gentiles should be admitted into the church, but on what terms they should be admitted – circumcised and following the law of Moses, or not. Once the decision had gone Paul's way, that law observance was not required, it was easier for Gentile converts to flow into the church. That debate about circumcision and the status of the law, however, was still a debate that was taking place within Jewish religion. Perhaps, with hindsight, the Council of Jerusalem made the later split into two religions inevitable but the separation did not happen in Paul's own lifetime. In the terms of his own time, he was a Christ-believing (messianic) Jew, not a Christian, strictly speaking. Historically, we can hardly identify Christianity as a religion independent of Judaism before Nero's persecution of the Christians after the fire in Rome in AD 64, and probably not before the destruction of the Jerusalem temple in AD 70, an event which was to radically change the character of Judaism. With the fire in Rome, Christianity was singled out as an identifiable group in the city, and by the time Rome destroyed the spiritual centre of Judaism a few years later, the Jewish Christians had already detached themselves from Jerusalem and moved out (tradition has it to Pella across the Jordan). By 64/70 Christianity had arrived, but not before. It is unlikely that anyone would have called Paul a Christian in his own lifetime. He was a Jew of a particular type.

Paul's Jewishness is important because, like Jesus, though in a slightly different way, he continued Jewish traditions but transformed our understanding of them, yet without ever repudiating them. His was a Judaism that centred on the faith of Abraham, not on the giving of the law at Sinai. He thought that Moses introduced only a temporary period in Jewish history – the time of the law – in which Jews would be saved by showing their faithfulness to God through law-observance. With the coming of Christ, faithfulness received a new object: Jesus Christ himself. Paul's version of Judaism was one that now incorporated all nations, and he found biblical precedents for this in scripture and in Isaiah and the Psalms in particular. His was a Judaism in which the scriptures (what Christians would later call the Old Testament) indicated God's plan for the salvation of the world and the basis on which that salvation would take place. The extent to which Paul used the scriptures to support his arguments shows how thoroughly Jewish he was. He knew much scripture by heart and expected his readers to be familiar with the texts too, which suggests that many and perhaps most of his original readers were either Jews or Gentile God-fearers who attended synagogue like Cornelius (Acts 10:2).

We should also consider here the question of how many of the letters collected in the New Testament actually come from Paul. Many academic books on Paul restrict their discussion to the seven definitely authentic letters: Romans, 1 and 2 Corinthians, Galatians, Philippians, Philemon and 1 Thessalonians. I will add 2 Thessalonians to that list and a respectable case can be made for Colossians, though I remain rather doubtful about that letter. The first to have been written was 1 Thessalonians, probably in AD 50, followed after only a few months by 2 Thessalonians. The first and second letters to Corinthians were written fairly close together around AD 54–55, but contain evidence of a more extensive correspondence between Paul and Corinth that has since disappeared. The original correspondence included an initial letter from Paul, which preceded our official No. 1, and another letter, written with 'anguish and tears', between Nos 1 and 2. Nor do we have the letters that the believers in Corinth wrote to Paul. One wonders how many more of Paul's letters might have gone missing! Galatians contains a preliminary run-through of Paul's ideas on justification, faith and works of the law, which he developed more fully in Romans. Again these letters come from the middle 50s. Philippians, possibly a combination of two or even three letters, was written from prison but we are not sure which one: probably Caesarea in AD 58 but possibly Rome in 61–62. We have no idea where the short letter to Philemon fits in, though it is related to one of Paul's imprisonments.

A comparison of the content and language of Colossians and Ephesians suggests they are by different authors and it is more likely that Paul wrote the former than the latter. Ephesians looks to me like a small compendium of Paul's thought culled from his authentic letters but published after his death. The arguments for Paul not having written the Pastoral Epistles (1 and 2 Timothy and Titus) are very weighty. These letters were written in Paul's name (pseudonymous authorship was a common biblical practice) and are from a later generation – AD 70–100 – but they show how Paul's influence was preserved to the end of the century in a number of schools associated with Paul and perhaps founded by him. To that extent it is reasonable to refer to them in a survey of Pauline thought, particularly where they continue Paul's own thinking, while bearing in mind that they may not come from his own hand.

The aim of this book is to allow Paul to speak for himself through extensive quotations and references. The meaning of Paul's theology is much disputed, now more than ever, but here I have for the most part avoided discussions with other Pauline scholars to help make his ideas accessible, so there are not many footnotes. What I have tried to do is to organise Paul's ideas around a particular topic: the Christian life. This offers one way around this complex, unsystematic, occasionally repetitive but remarkable thinker. His thought is rich and he has some wonderful passages – Romans 8:31–39 would be a reading for my funeral. My hope is that readers will turn to reading Paul himself. Even if it proves to be a struggle, it should be a rewarding one. He demands concentration, repeated reading and some understanding of his cultural and religious background. But Paul remains a great thinker for any age. And his message – the gospel – remains unbounded by any particular culture. In this he offers his readers an invitation to live a distinctive way of life.

1

Character

Rulebook Morality

There is a view, which may be considered to be a half-educated view, perhaps left over from childhood, that Christian morality involves slavishly following a code of rules. According to this view, the church has a fixed set of detailed prescriptions and prohibitions that have to be applied in the relevant circumstances to ensure the right outcomes. These rules may present themselves as having come directly from God, as do the Ten Commandments, or from the authority of the church in later centuries. However, this rule-bound morality is not the position of the New Testament and certainly not that of Paul.

It is true that both Jesus and Paul came from a religious tradition that valued law extremely highly. The Jewish scriptures contain several law books, each claiming to represent God's will, yet in reality these laws are part of a developing social morality that emerged over many centuries and that reflects changing historical and social circumstances. Consider, for example, the two sets of laws in Exodus 20:1–17 and 34:17–26. Each presents itself as the Ten Commandments given on Mount Sinai. Read them together and you will find that there are considerable differences between the two codes, so they cannot both be the original Ten Commandments. The texts themselves contain the clues to determine the historical period each comes from, though it is not our task to determine these here. Through these different stages of development God is presented in the Old Testament as a lawgiver who addresses his people through laws. Most people think of Old Testament law as apodictic law, i.e., negative imperative law ('you shall not ...'), but

7

most Old Testament law is actually casuistic, i.e., case law, what to do in particular circumstances ('if someone does such and such, you shall punish him by ...'). This is why there is so much of it as there are so many different cases to be covered, though the rabbis eventually simplified the multiplicity of Old Testament laws by organising it all into a code of 613 rules. These are meant to cover pretty much all the moral issues of life in the society for which they were written, even though many are actually technical rules for the ritual duties of the priests, such as we find in the Holiness Code (Leviticus 17—26). But as the laws are presented as coming from God, the synagogue sees their value to be timeless, so far as historical circumstances allow them to be carried out (i.e., there are no longer any animal sacrifices because there is no longer a temple). Atheists have great fun teasing those who want to follow everything in the Bible by reminding them, for example, of the demand to execute disobedient sons, female sorcerers and anyone who 'lies with an animal' (Exodus 22:18–19). While this is legitimate mockery of those who read historical texts unhistorically, the mockers might move on to the next few verses of Exodus 22, which are about the duty to protect foreign immigrants and the destitute.

When we trace the origin of these laws, we can see that they are by no means timeless or context free. The Old Testament itself describes occasions when new law scrolls appeared, occasions when the people of Israel had to do public penance before God for not having kept those laws, even though they had apparently known nothing about them. The best known example is the discovery of the scroll that, perhaps with some later expansion, became the Book of Deuteronomy, found when King Josiah was carrying out building work on the Jerusalem temple during his religious reform of the late seventh century BC (2 Kings 22:1—23:27). Another example is the law book that Ezra brought back to Jerusalem in the fourth century when he was sent from Babylon to take charge of the disorganised community in the ancient capital, a law book that had been preserved (or created) by the Jewish exiles in Babylon. It was Ezra's harsh administration that forced the men of Jerusalem to dismiss their foreign wives and mixed-race children and in doing so created a racially narrow view of what it was to be Jewish. (It should be added that there is an alternative and more humane understanding of what it is to belong to the people of God, expressed in Ruth and Jonah, which is sympathetic to faithful foreigners found among 'the nations'.) So Old Testament law is far from timeless; new laws appeared for new circumstances. The actual form that these laws took was determined by particular historical circumstances.

Moral Rules in the New Testament

By contrast, there are comparatively few moral rules to be found in the New Testament. The New Testament is in no sense a rule-book for life. Consider Jesus' approach in the Gospels. Given the mass of laws that a pious and literate Jew might be familiar with, it was of some general interest when a young scholar asked Jesus which is the greatest of them. Jesus' approach was to sum everything up by quoting Deuteronomy to the effect that legal observance is all about loving God and loving your neighbour (Mark 12:28–34, quoting Deuteronomy 6:4 and Leviticus 19:18). Those two lines sum it all up and make the rest, at one level, superfluous. When Jesus did give an instruction, as on divorce and remarriage (Mark 10:2–11), it is a rare example of him giving a rule and in this case it represents an interpretation of scripture (Deuteronomy 24:1–4 and Genesis 1:27) with a view to protecting married women who might be casually abandoned and made destitute if they were cast off in some arbitrary way by their husband. What Jesus does here is to shift the discourse from being about the minutiae of the conditions under which the more powerful figure could initiate a legal action – only men could bring divorce proceedings in Jewish law – to consider the consequences for the weaker partner, the woman.

Paul dealt with the law in an even more radical way. While Jesus gave interpretations to the law which were radically new (e.g. Matthew 5:21–48), he never said anything negative about the Torah. On the contrary, he was entirely positive in his appreciation of the law (Matthew 5:17–19; Mark 10:17–21). Paul is more ambiguous. Some of his remarks about the law are positive but his better known lines seem witheringly negative. His varied remarks on the law might suggest inconsistency, which would certainly make him difficult to understand and leave him open to different interpretations. His general comments about the law as a whole will be discussed later, but here our interest is in what he had to say about particular laws in order to focus on the issue of whether Paul held a legalistic morality.

Only infrequently does Paul offer his readers a moral law or a ruling. When he does he is careful to distinguish between his own opinion and the higher authority of Jesus, 'the Lord'. On the issue of marital separation and divorce, for example, an issue that had been raised by his correspondents in Corinth (1 Corinthians 7:1), Paul repeats the Lord's ruling, slightly expanded, that the husband and wife should not divorce; and if they separate, they should become reconciled or should remain unattached (7:10). For the rest, he gives his advice to Christians married to unbelievers that, if possible, they should not divorce or separate (women had the right to initiate divorce in Roman society, even if not under Jewish law) because the unbeliever and their children are made holy through the marriage to a Christian believer. Separation is possible, however, if the unbeliever makes life impossible for the Christian, because above all God has called us to peace (7:12–16). For the unmarried 'I have no command of the Lord, but I give my opinion as one who by the Lord's mercy is trustworthy' (7:25). He advises them to remain unmarried 'in view of the impending crisis' and because 'the appointed time has grown short' (7:26, 29). Remarks elsewhere in his letters show that Paul expected God's final judgement of the world to come very shortly, perhaps in his own lifetime, so he thought that concern with domestic matters, which are trivial by comparison, should not take over his readers' lives and so he, similarly, advises widows (and presumably widowers) not to remarry (7:39f). His concern with an impending cosmic judgement is a mark of how culture-bound and time-bound Paul's moral advice can sometimes be. His advice on marriage was only offered because the Christians in Corinth had requested it and Paul's response necessarily reflects their circumstances, but it does raise the question of how far Paul's particular ethical recommendations can be followed by later generations.

Take another case. Paul condemned a man in the community who was living with and presumably having sexual relations with his stepmother. Paul's judgement would have been based on Deuteronomy 22:30 which says that a man shall not marry his father's wife.

He was probably motivated in this judgement by a wish to escape criticism from the Jewish synagogue that the church's moral standards were scandalously lax (1 Corinthians 5:1–5). (Given the general moral standards of the city, it is unlikely that many pagans would have been bothered.) Paul was certainly concerned about the sexual behaviour of his fellow Christians, especially those in Corinth and Rome, yet his advice on fornication, while strict, is fairly general. The one occasion when he gave a particular rule in this area was never to take a prostitute (1 Corinthians 6:15f).

It was in Corinth that these matters came to the surface, a cosmopolitan port with a range of state-approved and innovative cults. As a pious Jew, Paul's prime concern was that the believers in Corinth should not be drawn into idolatry, which he considered to be the source of all evil (see Romans 1:18–32 which is Paul's rewrite of Wisdom 13—14 where a similarly hard line is taken against idolatry). In 1 Corinthians 10, Paul recalls the disaster that came upon those Jews who worshipped the golden image of the calf in Exodus 32 as an example of the consequences of idolatry. But his particular advice in this letter is not about the worship of idols, which is obviously out of the question for a Christian believer, but about eating food that had been ritually offered to pagan gods, which could be found on open sale in the marketplace. He thought the Jewish prohibition of certain foods, as set out in Leviticus, no longer applied and he himself now felt free to eat anything. He thought followers of Christ did not have to be concerned about any of the food they were offered, whether in the market or at the dinner table. On the other hand, 'all things are lawful but not all things are beneficial' because of the religious sensibilities of some of the believers in the community who wanted no suspicion of contact with idolatry at all. These are the ones that Paul calls the 'weak in faith' in Romans 14:1. So while Paul himself felt free to eat anything, he was prepared to abstain from eating meat for fear of unsettling anyone who was worried that it might have been tainted by pagan priests (1 Corinthians 8). So the ancient rules have been suspended but religious sensitivity demands that old practices have to be respected.

Does Paul have any more rules? He instructs his readers in 2 Corinthians 12:21 not to lie to one another, but that is an unexceptionable rule. What still causes some difficulty is his body of instructions on how the Christian community in Rome should relate to the state (Romans 13). Be subject to the governing authorities, he says, 'Pay to all what is due to them – taxes to whom taxes are due, revenue to whom revenue is due, respect to whom respect is due, honour to whom honour is due.' There have been historical moments when such deference to the state has proved to be a particular problem. Should one remain a law-abiding subject, as Romans 13 suggests, under a totalitarian government that is responsible for major crimes, as in Germany in the 1940s or in South Africa under apartheid and in so many other places and situations? Should one remain a law-abiding subject in any state that is unjust? If one thinks that every word of scripture must be obeyed as it stands, the answer must be 'yes', and one must go along with Paul's view that 'those authorities … have been instituted by God … For rulers are not a terror to good conduct but to bad … [They are] the servant of God to execute wrath on the wrongdoer.' And this was written during the reign of the appalling (and terrifying) Nero! Paul seems to be telling us that we must obey the state no matter how dreadful its ruler. By way of mitigation, we should point to the context in which the Letter to the Romans was written. It was probably written between AD 56 and 58 when Nero, as a youth, was still behaving himself – more or less. Nero became emperor in 54 when he was only 16 and Rome was effectively ruled for a time by his mother Agrippina and his tutor Seneca. The first five years of his reign was known as the Quinquennium and it was a period of unusual calm. In fact things stayed generally peaceful until AD 61 as Nero played the part of Augustus, despite a few murders along the way, including that of his mother. After he had deposed the senate in AD 62, however, Nero's rule became vicious and unpredictable. Had Paul written Romans close to the end of his life, he might have had a less benign view of the state and he might have offered more tempered advice to his fellow citizens.

A word should be added about the so-called *Haustafeln* or domestic instructions of Colossians 3:18—4:1 and Ephesians 5:21—6:9 which, although Pauline in a broad sense, probably did not come from Paul himself and look rather like conventional Stoic morality. These instructions are about the reciprocal relations between husbands and wives, parents and children, and slaves and their masters. Each of them must be kind, loving and respectful of the other, but the inferior partner (as seen at that time) – the wife, the child and the slave – must show obedience. The author gives no hint of social revolution here, but then nor did anyone else at that time, pagan or Christian. There was no hint, for example, that slavery might be a bad thing – more on this later.

Such, then, is the extent of Paul's particular instructions on how Christians should behave. They do not amount to much and are far from being a comprehensive guide to life. On these occasions he was often responding to questions put to him about issues that concerned his correspondents rather than initiating general instructions, so his advice tends to be context-bound and not necessarily for all times and all places. Even though his letters have been canonised by the church as scripture, they remain social products. It is clear that one can in no sense construct a rule-book for Christian behaviour from Paul's letters. Certainly he has a lot to say about morals and what he says is often delivered with passion, but his ethics cannot be described as a 'law ethics' despite what you might have expected from his Jewish background. Paul's ethics is about something else. He prefers to talk about character: the character you once were and the character you should become.

Paul's Ethics

The etymology of the word suggests that ethics is about habits, and that is what Paul deals with: patterns of behaviour that have been acquired and become second nature. On several occasions he offers lists of habits to be avoided and habits to be cultivated. In the lists of things to be avoided Paul seems to be describing the actual behaviour of his fellow Christians before the 'new life' that comes with baptism (Romans 6:4). There are three such lists in the letters to Corinth and these refer to: fornicators, idolaters, adulterers, male prostitutes, sodomites, thieves, the greedy, drunkards, revilers, robbers – none of whom, we are told, will inherit the kingdom of God – 'and this is what some of you used to be' (1 Corinthians 6:9–11). He tells his readers to mix no longer with such people (5:11). In his next letter he adds to the list the vices of: quarrelling, jealousy, anger, selfishness, slander, gossip, conceit and creating disorder. And finally he adds the more general traits of impurity, sexual immorality and licentiousness, which may all come to the same thing – he is not precise about what they are exactly (2 Corinthians 12:20–21).

He tells the Thessalonians that greed and looking for flattery and praise are to be avoided. He says that when he first came to Thessalonica he made no such imposition on them. He might have made demands on them as an apostle, but he claims that he dealt with them gently as a nurse would with children in her care (1 Thessalonians 2:5–8). In all this Paul does not impose rules but tries to act as a model for what it is to live the Christian life.

Sexual immorality among his charges was a preoccupation for Paul, and no doubt there was good reason for this – there seems to have been plenty of it about in the cities of the Empire. He refers to it a number of times: in 1 Corinthians 5:9–11; 6:9; 2 Corinthians 12:21; Galatians 5:19; and 1 Thessalonians 4:3–5, though always in rather general terms. In these places Paul maintains the moral outlook of the Torah, though without spelling out details of particular acts, with the exception of Romans 1:26–27, which includes a condemnation of homosexuality, reflecting Leviticus 20:13 with its roots in the destruction of the city of Sodom (Genesis 19).[1] Here at the beginning of Romans, Paul continued the legal-moral tradition that he inherited from Judaism and applied it to the whole human race. The first chapter focuses on Gentiles and Paul lays it on pretty thick about how wicked they are:

> They [are] filled with every kind of wickedness, evil, covetousness, malice. Full of envy, murder, strife, deceit, craftiness, they are gossips, slanderers, God-haters, insolent, haughty, boastful, inventors of evil, rebellious towards parents, foolish, faithless, heartless, ruthless. They know God's decree, that those who practise such things deserve to die – yet they not only do them but even applaud others who practise them. (Romans 1:29–32)

---

1 This condemnation of homosexuality is not much repeated in the Old Testament and it may represent an 'idealised' priestly condemnation, so to speak, that may not have been imposed often or even at all in ancient Israel.

It is hard to believe that all Gentiles could have been so bad but in Paul's scheme they all deserve the wrath of God and condemnation is coming their way.

In the next chapter Paul turns his attention to those Jews who believe they will escape condemnation because they are members of God's elect people and custodians of his law. Knowing the requirements of God's law allows Jews to judge other people – to be a guide to the blind, a light to those in darkness, a corrector of the foolish, and a teacher of children – but not if they break those same laws themselves. Paul's examples are stealing, adultery and robbing pagan temples (2:17–24). His warning for the Jews is quite as strong as for the Gentiles. The issue is not whether one is Jewish or not, it is one's moral character, for 'a person is a Jew who is one inwardly … it is spiritual and not literal' (2:29). It seems that at this point of his argument the whole of humanity is culpable, Jew and Gentile with no exceptions, and everyone is destined to receive the wrath of God.

However, in general, Paul's account of moral character is far from negative. His lists of characteristics to be avoided are balanced by corresponding lists of qualities to be cultivated. And while in practice Paul more frequently lists vices, each of Paul's vices implies an opposite virtue. The full list is: Virtues: 2 Corinthians 6:6; Galatians 5:22–24; Philippians 4:8; Colossians 3:12–17; and perhaps Romans 12:4–21, from which a list of moral virtues can be extracted. Vices: Romans 1:29–31; 13:13; 1 Corinthians 5:10–11; 6:9–10; 2 Corinthians 12:20–21; Galatians 5:19–21; and Colossians 3:5–9.

Virtues and vices are not usually placed one immediately after the other but they are in Galatians, which is a good place to see how they match up. There Paul tells his readers to 'Live by the spirit … and do not gratify the desires of the flesh' (5:16), where desires of the flesh are not sexual desires particularly but desires that contrast more generally with living by the spirit (or Spirit). 'Fleshly desires' are what characterise life before baptism, though Paul is enough of a realist to know that unspiritual habits can continue after baptism. He then gives his examples:

> Now the works of the flesh are obvious: fornication, impurity, licentiousness, idolatry, sorcery, enmities, strife, jealousy, an-

ger, quarrels, dissensions, factions, envy, drunkenness, carous-
ing, and things like these. (Galatians 5:19–21)

He immediately contrasts them with what characterises the Christian life:

> By contrast, the fruit of the Spirit is love, joy, peace, patience,
> kindness, generosity, faithfulness, gentleness, and self-control.
> There is no law against such things. (5:22–23)

And in cultivating these habits, we have to resist becoming con-
ceited, which may come through envying or competing with one
another (v. 26).

Paul adds to this list of what in other letters he calls fruits of the
Spirit. In 2 Corinthians he commends himself to his readers
through what he has had to endure in bringing the gospel to them
and in the moral qualities he has tried to exemplify for them: purity,
knowledge, patience, kindness, holiness of spirit, genuine love and
truthful speech, while always tolerating calumnies and injustices
(6:6f). One chapter later, he praises the generous support of the
community in Macedonia at a time when he was reluctant to
impose himself on the Corinthians for his daily needs. So Paul can
tell the Philippians, 'Brothers and sisters, join in imitating me, and
observe those who live according to the example you have in us'
(Philippians 3:17). In a typically Pauline way, the author of Colossians, hoping to be accepted as a model of exemplary behaviour, tells
his readers to

> clothe yourselves with compassion, kindness, humility, meek-
> ness and patience. Bear with one another and, if anyone has a
> complaint against another, forgive each other; just as the
> Lord has forgiven you, so you also must forgive. Above all,
> clothe yourselves with love, which binds everything together
> in perfect harmony. (Colossians 3:12–14)

The author of 1 Timothy adds, 'pursue righteousness, godliness,
faith, love, endurance, gentleness' (1 Timothy 6:11). His readers

must be trustworthy in all things (1 Corinthians 4:2). And the author of Ephesians writes,

> Clothe yourselves with the new self, created according to the likeness of God in true righteousness and holiness. So then, putting away falsehood, let all of us speak the truth to our neighbours, for we are members of one another. Be angry but do not sin [referring to Psalm 4:4]; do not let the sun go down on your anger, and do not make room for the devil. Thieves must give up stealing; rather let them labour and work honestly with their own hands, so as to have something to share with the needy. Let no evil talk come out of your mouths, but only what is useful for building up, as there is need, so that your words may give grace to those who hear … Put away from you all bitterness and wrath and anger and wrangling and slander, together with all malice, and be kind to one another, tender-hearted, forgiving one another, as God in Christ has forgiven you. (Ephesians 4:24–32)

For a work of 16 chapters, Romans does not seem much concerned with behaviour. But in chapter 12 Paul focuses on activities that are typical of life within the church and how they should be carried out: prophets, ministers, teachers and exhorters should prophesy, minister, teach and exhort in proportion to their faith; 'the giver' should give 'in generosity; the leader, in diligence; the compassionate, in cheerfulness' (Romans 12:6–8). Paul then lists those virtues that lead to action:

> Let love be genuine; hate what is evil, hold fast to what is good; love one another with mutual affection; outdo one another in showing honour. Do not lag in zeal, be ardent in spirit, serve the Lord. Rejoice in hope, be patient in suffering, persevere in prayer. Contribute to the needs of the saints; extend hospitality to strangers. (Romans 12:9–13)

Finally in verses 14–21 he tells them to bless those who have wronged them and not curse them; live in harmony with one another by sharing each others' laughter and tears; not to be haughty or claim to be wiser than they are; never to take revenge; for 'if your enemies are hungry, feed them; if they are thirsty, give them something to drink ... Do not be overcome by evil, but overcome evil with good.' This was advice he had first given to the Thessalonians (1 Thessalonians 5:16).

Philippians has a rather different emphasis from Romans and is a mature letter that is principally about behaviour, but it also incorporates an explicit spirituality and Christology to underpin its morality. This letter tells us to be pure and blameless (Colossians 1:22 says 'holy and blameless and irreproachable') and to live a life worthy of the gospel (1:10, 27). We should look to the interests of others before our own (2:4). Paul's readers should avoid murmuring and arguing, 'so that you may be blameless and innocent, children of God without blemish in the midst of a crooked and perverse generation, in which you shine like stars in the world' (2:15), a wonderful line appropriate for any generation. We are told that our gentleness should be known to everyone and that we should remain content with whatever we have in life (4:5, 11). The seriousness of this is clear when Paul tells his readers that they have to work out their salvation in fear and trembling (2:12). He ends by telling them to keep in mind all those things that are honourable and virtuous, and to 'keep on doing the things you have learned and received and heard and seen in me, and the God of peace will be with you' (4:9). What we have in Paul's ethics, then, is not a code of rules but a focus on the human person as a moral agent, and in Paul himself a model of what the Christian life might look like. And supporting that, as we shall see, is the moral foundation of Jesus Christ himself who took on the form of a slave, emptied himself and died on a cross.

Character not Law

Paul, then, presents his readers with a morality centred on the idea of character. The Greek for 'character' is *dokimē*. This is a word that does not occur much in Paul or the New Testament generally. Words in Greek from the same root (*dok-*) have the sense of being tested and approved, which leads to the sense of one having been formed with the right character. So when 2 Timothy 2:15 says 'Do your best to present yourself to God as one approved by him' the author is urging his readers to have the kind of character that will be approved – tested and approved! The only occasion in Paul where it is necessary to translate *dokimē* as 'character' is when he tells us that our sufferings produce endurance, endurance produces character (i.e., the character that will be approved by God), and character produces hope – approved at the present time and to be vindicated in the future (Romans 5:3–5).

In some ways Paul gives us an idealised picture of moral and spiritual development, doubtless to encourage his communities, who were small groups in what could be an antagonistic world. In practice, standards were not always the best in those churches. We know from his difficult relationship with some of those in Corinth that their behaviour fell far below his expectations, and in some respects his own behaviour fell below what they expected. When the Ephesians were told that the thieves among them should stop stealing, it is clear that there must have been ongoing problems with pilfering in that small community. And when the author of 1 Timothy outlines the qualities looked for in bishops, elders/ presbyters and deacons ('not a drunkard, not violent but gentle, not quarrelsome and not a lover of money', 1 Timothy 3:3) it looks as though some of their appointments had not turned out well. People's behaviour rarely turns out as well as we hope.

This focus of Paul on character accords well with virtue ethics, a style of ethics that goes back to ancient Greece and is experiencing something of a revival at the present time. One of the earliest writers on ethics was Aristotle and he thought that the goal of life was to become virtuous, because a virtuous man would live a good life, would do the right things, would flourish and achieve *eudaimonia* (often translated 'happiness' but actually meaning something more like 'well-being'). One of the difficulties with Aristotle's version of virtue ethics is that it is elitist. The only people who could in practice become virtuous were men: men who were of independent means with full political rights, supported by a family and slaves to free them from domestic concerns. Such was the life of the philosopher of that time: virtuous and free. So it was Aristotle who established the main features of virtue ethics, which were that human life has an end or goal (a *telos*), the end is *eudaimonia*/well-being, and to achieve this state of well-being a man must first become a virtuous or good person. It is an ethics that focuses on character, so having a virtuous character is what leads finally to well-being or living well. This is a style of ethics that is about moral growth, moving by stages towards a state of virtue, while never expecting to achieve it perfectly. One can always go further.

Human development is a matter of the intellect, of course, but it is also about emotional education. It is not rule-based but it is to be practised and perfected like learning a craft or improving skills in a sport. Good habits are to be learnt and role-models imitated (e.g. Jesus and Paul). The moral life is like being an artist; the good life comes from practice and competence.

Thomas Aquinas is credited with having developed virtue ethics into something more socially inclusive than Aristotle managed. St Thomas located ethics within a specifically Christian context and determined that the final end of all human life was what he called the 'beatific vision', the vision of God that one would share with the angels and the saints (for the medieval Christian that is what it was to be a saint: one who is in the presence of God). As a Christian theologian, Thomas believed in God's grace – which he defined at its simplest as *auxilium Dei*, the assistance of God – and he realised that the final aim of the virtuous life could not be simply the result of human effort and achievement. Christian ethics is never about pulling yourself up by your own bootstraps. Through grace a person moves from what they are to what they might become and in doing so they realise ever more fully what it is to be human – with God's assistance.

While virtue ethics received its classic Christian expression in the thirteenth century, the last two or three decades have seen it have a considerable revival of interest.[2] Whether in Aristotle's or Thomas's form, it runs counter to many trends that have been prominent in moral philosophy over the past couple of centuries, post-Enlightenment trends that have been predominantly secular. Virtue ethics attempts to find a way between ethics that are rule-based and

---

2   This revival is associated with authors such as Alasdair MacIntyre, Stanley Hauerwas, Nancy Sherman, Philippa Foot, Jean Porter and James Keenan. Joseph J. Kotva Jr, *The Christian Case for Virtue Ethics* (Washington DC: Georgetown University Press, 1996) is a useful introduction.

related to the notion of duty, and those that focus on outcomes. The former can be identified with Old Testament ethics and Kant, and the latter with Mill, Bentham and Utilitarianism. It is also an ethics that refuses to fall into subjectivism or moral relativism, where deciding what is good becomes arbitrary and whatever an individual happens to think it is.

Paul was not a moral philosopher or a moral theologian, in the sense that he was not trying to lay down a rational foundation for a moral theory. He was, in the first place, a missionary and a letter-writer. He did not teach in an academy or yeshiva (Jewish school or seminary); he preached in houses and in synagogues and in the open air. What he says in his letters about how people should conduct their lives is usually written in terms of what kind of people they should be (or not be), and in this regard his ethics are consonant with what we know as virtue ethics. His writings promote a version of ethics where human *being* precedes human *doing*. There are certain particularities to Paul's ethics. Virtues are to be practised as ends in themselves and not merely as a means to some higher end, whether it be prosperity, social esteem or eternal life. But Paul first presented his lists of virtues in a particular context, which is as a preparation for life with God after judgement and resurrection. One of the things he believed resurrection would bring is a divine transformation so that one would become Christlike, but first one has to be fit for it. Being virtuous on earth is the Christian's first aim but it is not the final expectation; already 'our citizenship is in heaven' (Philippians 3:20) but his readers were not yet there. Making oneself fit for such a destiny involves moral growth; we have to 'strain forward to what lies ahead' (Philippians 3:13). Bad behaviour towards or with others will drag us back (see Galatians 5:19–21). Moral growth is at the same time social growth, hence Paul's use of 'body' language, which we shall look at later, to characterise interdependency within the community. This is a form of ethics which starts with a focus on individual character but always within the context of support in a community. And it is just as much about spirituality – the divine and the human working together. Paul was far from being systematic or exhaustive in his letters and we might ourselves want to include other virtues if we reckon Paul has omitted any. But Paul does not have to be exhaustive in this ethics. It is enough for him to say,

> Finally, beloved, whatever is true, whatever is honourable, whatever is just, whatever is pure, whatever is pleasing, whatever is commendable, if there is any excellence [*aretē*, virtue] and if there is anything worthy of praise, think about these things. (Philippians 4:8)

What follows in this book is an account, chapter by chapter, of the virtues that, according to Paul, make up the character of those who aspire to live the Christian life.

2

Humility

Boasting in the Lord

Paul had a particular preoccupation with boasting. Boasting is a theme that runs through several of his letters: Romans, 1 and 2 Corinthians, Philippians, with a brief mention in Galatians and reaching its climax in 2 Corinthians. It is a theme which, if we pursue it, helps to explain one important aspect of his theology, that of humility.

Some of the Christians in Corinth had accused Paul of boasting and lording it over them (2 Corinthians 1:24). The background to this accusation lies in the nature of the church in Corinth. The Christian community in Corinth in the 50s cannot have contained more than a few dozen members but already a number of factions had formed, each of which claimed their own leader. Some looked to Paul, others to Apollos, Cephas/Peter and, rather bizarrely coming after those three, Christ (1 Corinthians 1:11–12). Paul's response was to tell them never to boast about human leaders (3:21) because they belong entirely to God, for God has given them everything: 'life, death, the present, the future – all belong to you.' The forming of factions and boasting about superiority are inappropriate and irrelevant. However, the problem did not go away and by the time Paul got to the end of his Second Letter, he was writing assertively, even aggressively, about the fault of boasting because some of those in Corinth had turned the charge against him. By this stage they had clearly got under his skin with the charge of boasting as their exchange became increasingly acrimonious. And, because of the way Paul tried to defend himself, you might think that there was some justification for their accusation.

23

We do not know how the dispute began because we do not have the first letter that Paul wrote to Corinth (there is a passing reference to this missing letter in 1 Corinthians 5:9). The suggestion that Paul had been lording it over them may have come from a misreading of the long section 1 Corinthians 1:10—4:21, which describes the Christians in Corinth as being a poor lot by worldly standards: 'not many of you were wise by human standards, not many were powerful, not many were of noble birth' (1:26). Paul used this to show how in Christ, God had raised up the foolish and powerless, but the Corinthians might have thought that Paul was trying to undermine their worldly self-confidence and was setting himself above their apparently modest level. Certainly Paul makes much of their low estate: 'God chose what is foolish ... God chose what is weak ... God chose what is low and despised in the world ... so that no one might boast in the presence of God' (1:27–29). He calls them infants who are not yet ready for solid food (3:1–2). The allegation that they lacked worldly wisdom (3:18) would certainly have caused resentments among his readers in Corinth. Paul could be seen to be getting above himself. His purpose, of course, was to make it clear that the important things of life all come, not from human achievement, but from grace, the free assistance of God.

> He [God] is the source of your life in Christ Jesus, who became for us wisdom from God, and righteousness and sanctification and redemption, in order that, as it is written [perhaps an allusion to the Greek of Jeremiah 9:23–24, but not in fact a quotation from there], 'Let the one who boasts, boast in the Lord.' (1:30–31)

But he seems to have left them with a different impression.

Already towards the end of this First Letter, Paul had to defend himself by stating that he does not boast before God of his own achievements but of them, the community he had founded (15:31). He repeated this several times in the Second Letter (2 Corinthians 1:12; 7:4, 14; 8:24; 9:3). His defence was that his pride was not in himself but in them, and in the same way they, by association, could boast of whatever graces had been given to Paul (1:14; 5:12).

Nevertheless, there persisted a perceived slight – Paul making himself superior to them.

A careful reading of 2 Corinthians will show that Paul was actually quite upset by all this and no doubt depressed by it too. This is particularly clear in the last chapters 10—13. These have a tone markedly different from the first nine chapters, which has led some to suggest that they might come from a separate letter, maybe part of the missing letter that he wrote 'out of much distress and anguish of heart and with many tears' that preceded our 2 Corinthians (2 Corinthians 2:4). What we are not sure of is whether these unsettling chapters come from the middle of the correspondence or as a climax to it. Was there any final reconciliation?

First, let us consider Paul's depressive state: he speaks of the affliction he experienced in Asia where he was so 'utterly, unbearably crushed' that he despaired of life itself (1:8). Later he speaks of being subject to a severe ordeal of affliction (8:2), of being downcast but consoled by Titus. In two separate passages he lists how he has been affected for ill but how he has not bowed under pressure. He says that he is afflicted in every way, perplexed, persecuted, struck down, 'always carrying in the body the death of Jesus', yet he is not crushed or driven to despair, not forsaken or destroyed (4:8–10). And later in 6:8ff he writes of suffering the indignity of being treated as an impostor even though he is true, as unknown though he is well known, as being as good as dead while being fully alive, as punished yet not destroyed, as full of sorrow while in reality being joyful, as poverty-stricken while making many joyful, and as having nothing while believing he possessed everything that is of worth. If ever a man was misjudged and mistreated, he seems to be telling us, it was he. There is a great deal of rhetoric here, of course, but in order to understand this letter it is important to realise that he was being ground down by a variety of pressures, enough to bring on depression in even the most resilient of men. If he insists that he does not lose heart (4:1), it is precisely because he might very easily have done so.

This is the letter in which he particularly emphasises the sufferings he continued to undergo in his life as an apostle. The well-known list of his imprisonments, floggings, beatings, a stoning and shipwrecks appears at 11:23ff; the dangers he experienced while travelling; the hunger, thirst, anxiety and exhaustion. Of course, he also mentions consolation and the confidence that he places in God of eventual vindication (1:10, 21; 3:4f), even though it is hard to take him at his word when he says that he is actually overjoyed in all this affliction (7:4). The thing that really seems to have upset Paul, however, more than conventional hardships no matter how severe they were, was the charge from those in the Corinthian church that he habitually boasted of his achievements and that he looked down on them. We feel the strength of his reaction to this in chapters 10—12.

Why this unpleasantness upset him so much is something we shall look at in a moment, but first let us examine the charge itself. That there was something in the charge can be sensed when Paul asks his readers at 3:1 whether he is beginning to commend himself again, even though he insists that he is not (5:12). What was it that he might have been boasting about? First, his authority. He says that if perhaps he has boasted of his authority too much, he is not ashamed because he has been given it by the Lord in order to build up the community in Corinth, a community which after all he had founded himself (10:8). Second, his descent as a child of Abraham. Here he seems to be holding his position against 'false apostles':

> But whatever anyone dares to boast of – I am speaking as a fool now – I also dare to boast of that. Are they Hebrews? So am I. Are they Israelites? So am I. Are they descendants of Abraham? So am I. (11:21f)

Third, that he had endured more than others in his efforts to promote the Christian gospel. And it is at this point that Paul introduces the list of his past hardships that has already been referred to above and that reaches the conclusion: 'Are they ministers of Christ? I am talking like a madman – I am a better one.' Fourth, that God had given him ecstatic experiences:

> It is necessary to boast: there is nothing to be gained by it, but I will go on to visions and revelations of the Lord. I know a person in Christ [presumably Paul himself] who fourteen years ago [this would have been around AD 40] was caught up

to the third heaven … And I know that such a person … was caught up into Paradise and heard things that are not to be told, that no mortal is permitted to repeat. On behalf of such a one I will boast, but on my own behalf I will not boast, except of my weaknesses. (12:1–5)

Who were the ministers of Christ in 2 Corinthians 11:23 that Paul compares himself to? They are those he ironically calls 'super-apostles'. He admits that he is less impressive as a speaker (11:6), unprepossessing in appearance (10:10), but he is superior in knowledge because of what God has revealed to him. The credit for this goes to God, however, not himself. He never names the super-apostles but Paul suggests that they have introduced another Jesus to Corinth, so that the Corinthians have now submitted to a gospel different from the one they first accepted from Paul. The 'different gospel' in Galatians is that of the Judaisers who wanted to impose the Mosaic law, specifically circumcision and the food laws, on all Christian believers alike, Jew and Gentile. Was this the problem in Corinth? We cannot be sure but Paul certainly had to assert his authority against those super-apostles and, as he sees it, their false gospel. This may have been seen as a form of boasting but in the end Paul could only allow himself to boast of what he had received from God. Whatever we may regard as his achievements, achievements that we might even think heroic, Paul feels obliged to leave them out of consideration *as achievements*. He boasts, if it counts as boasting at all, of his weakness and his inability to avoid suffering, for it is a paradox of Christian belief that God turns weakness and suffering into strength and power – though not worldly power.

He [God] said to me, 'My grace is sufficient for you, for power is made perfect in weakness.' So, I will boast all the more gladly of my weaknesses, so that the power of Christ may dwell in me. Therefore I am content with weaknesses, insults, hardships, persecutions, and calamities for the sake of Christ; for whenever I am weak, then I am strong. (12:9–10)

Paul always seems to be on the defensive in this exchange, which may explain his prickly behaviour and the vigour of his rebuttal of the charge laid against him. The heavy irony when he refers to himself in 11:19 as a fool and when he tells his readers that 'you gladly put up with fools, being wise yourselves' reminds one of the bitterness that you find in Galatians 5:12 when Paul, using a heavy-handed pun, wishes that those Christian Judaisers who pressed for the circumcision (*peritomē*) of Gentile believers should themselves be prepared to slice off (*katatomē*) everything! Paul was not always the most sensitive of correspondents. While it is clear that he was particularly sensitive to the accusation of boasting, he does seem to have had a form of justifiable pride, though in relatively small things. He accepted support from fellow believers in Macedonia and was proud of not having been a financial burden on the community in Corinth. He expressed pride in the community he had founded there (1 Corinthians 15:31; 2 Corinthians 1:14; 7:4, 14; 8:24; 9:3). On the other hand, this repeated expression of pride in the Corinthians eventually comes to sound like special pleading to win over a community that he was finding especially difficult. However, he said the same of the churches of Macedonia, Thessalonica and Philippi, so no doubt he really meant it.

The issue of boasting that came to a head in Corinth also has traces in Paul's other major letters, though without having the same edge. He says Jews may boast of their closeness to God and their possession of the law but not of being a Jew, for that is an inward, spiritual matter in which one 'receives praise not from others but from God' (Romans 2:17, 29). The only boasting that is permissible, and one that is actually to be recommended in spiritual matters, is proclaiming what God has brought about in Christ, and this is not boasting on one's own behalf at all:

> In Christ Jesus, then, I have reason to boast of my work for God. For I will not venture to speak of anything except what Christ has accomplished through me to win obedience from the Gentiles, by word and deed, by the power of signs and wonders, by the power of the Spirit of God. (Romans 15:17–19; see also 5:11 and Philippians 1:26; 3:3)

While it might be tempting to boast of one's own achievements, there is no question that Paul disapproved of it. Of the super-apostles he says, 'such boasters are false apostles, deceitful workers, disguising themselves as apostles of Christ' (2 Corinthians 11:13). The real problem in this context is those apostles who take the credit for work done by other people, in this case Paul himself. He is clear that no one should boast in the presence of God and he twice produces the maxim 'Let the one who boasts, boast in the Lord' (1 Corinthians 1:29–31 and 2 Corinthians 10:17). His final word on this is, 'May I never boast of anything except the cross of our Lord Jesus Christ, by which the world has been crucified to me and I to the world' (Galatians 6:14).

Being Humble-Minded

Whether or not Paul was really guilty as charged, we have to ask ourselves why boasting raised such a passion in Paul in that final section of 2 Corinthians. It was surely because boasting is the enemy of that most fundamental of Christian virtues: humility. The word used by Paul for 'humble' is *tapeinos*. There is an initial problem here because the English words 'humble' and 'humility' tend to suggest feelings or dispositions rather than actions. And they have become rather negative words because of their associations with putting on a grovelling and hypocritical demeanour. Nineteenth-century literature – we think of Dickens – portrays self-consciously humble men whom you would not trust with your life savings. In Greek the concept has more to do with your status in society. In the Graeco-Roman world there was an elite of noble-born, educated, free and wealthy, virtuous men who were worthy of society's praise. And there were the rest, the common people, of no particular rank, who were the humble (*tapeinoi,* Latin: *humiles*). To recommend in that culture that someone should be humble was to encourage them not only to think and feel in a certain way, not only to be deferential, but also to knowingly take up a low position in society. It involved shedding wealth and becoming obedient and of service to others, acting as though others were higher up the social chain than you. To have recommended this in the ancient world as an act of virtue would have been preposterous because the word had entirely negative associations. In no way would one envy the low-born. Only before the gods should the high-born be humble.[1]

Things were seen rather differently in Jewish culture. God makes rich and makes poor; he raises men up and puts them down (1 Samuel 2:6f). Humility is here accepting your allotted place in the world. Like Job, you should take everything that God throws at you, good and bad, blessing and curse. Yet in the eighth century BC Amos was not so passive. He saw that the impoverished were made so by the rich and powerful. Amos brought social and political criticism to ancient Jewish society, not just a fatalistic acceptance of the status quo. Amos denounced the wicked for their exploitation of the humble and proclaimed the God of Israel to be a God who demanded protection for the poor of the land. This political radicalism was later psychologised in Proverbs so that now it is the rich who should become humble by showing modesty before the lower class, without themselves actually ceasing to be rich. You can still be rich but you must not flaunt it. It is the arrogant who will be destroyed and the modest/humble who will receive honour, an attitude which is particularly marked in the apocryphal book of Jesus ben Sira (Ecclesiasticus). Here everyone has to be humble no matter what their position in society, for it is mutuality that ensures basic social justice, though even this falls short of an equality of wealth and status. True social equality seems to have been best exemplified in second-temple Judaism by the community at Qumran by the Dead Sea, if Pliny is to be believed.[2]

A major shift in this tradition is indicated in the prophecy of Zechariah 9:9 that

> your king comes to you;
> triumphant and victorious is he,
> humble and riding on a donkey,
> on a colt, the foal of a donkey.

Here it is prophesied that the anointed king of Israel will adopt a position of humility, practical humility, even though, as king, he is

---

1   Klaus Wengst, *Humility: Solidarity of the Humiliated* (London: SCM Press, 1988), pp. 4–15.
2   Wengst, *Humility*, pp. 16–35.

to rule. This is the prophecy that Jesus acted out at his entry into the royal city but for him it had already become a whole pattern of life, which in turn meshed with his teaching about God's promised reversal of social positions:

> For all who exalt themselves will be humbled, and those who humble themselves will be exalted. (Luke 14:11; 18:14; Matthew 23:12)

> But many who are first will be last, and the last will be first. (Mark 10:31; Matthew 19:30; 20:16; Luke 13:30)

So, what of Paul? We have seen his strong line on boasting. To contrast with boasting, he lists humility among the positive virtues: 'clothe yourselves with compassion, kindness, humility, meekness and patience' (Colossians 3:12 and adapted in Ephesians 4:2). It is Philippians that is the central location for what Paul has to say on humility, a letter written in the latter part of his life while he was in prison.[3] The key passage is 2:1–11. Paul first looks for spiritual unity. He urges his readers to make his joy complete by being 'of the same mind' (*to auto phronēte*), 'of one mind' (*to hen phronountes*). This was a community with whom Paul had an excellent relationship, who supported him materially and spiritually even while he was staying in Corinth trying to sort out that troublesome church. So urging them to unity and like-mindedness can hardly have been a problem. But what is this mindedness that they should share? It is humble-mindedness:

> Do nothing from selfish ambition or conceit, but in humility (*tapeinophrosunē*) regard others as better than yourselves. Let each of you look not to your own interests, but to the interests of others. (2:3–4)

He then asks them to have the same mindedness that Christ had (2:4), which he extrapolates in the well-known hymn that follows

---

3 John Reumann, *Philippians*, The Anchor Yale Bible (New Haven and London: Yale University Press, 2008), pp. 6–13.

(2:5–11). It is not clear whether Paul is the author of this or whether it was already established in the early Christian liturgy but its author has given it a particular poetic structure. It is in two contrasting strophes. Each strophe is in three parts that build on each other. The first is about humiliation: Jesus did not cling to equality with God; he emptied himself and became a slave; and as a man he humbled himself in obedience even to death on a cross. The second is about a consequent exaltation: God gave him a name above all others; every knee will bend at the name of Jesus; and every tongue shall confess that he is Lord (*kurios*).

Let us focus on the first strophe:

[Let the same mind be in you that was in Christ Jesus]
who, though he was in the form of God, did not regard
    equality with God as something to be exploited,
but emptied himself [*heauton ekenōsen*] taking the form of a
    slave, being born in human likeness.
And being found in human form, he humbled himself
    [*etapeinōsen heauton*] and became obedient to the point of
    death – even death on a cross.

This mindedness that the Christians in Philippi share with Paul and with Christ leads to action. Humility (*tapeinōsis*) for Christ meant becoming human, becoming a slave and dying on a cross, and this is the foundation and model for humility in Christian life. A little further into the letter Paul asks the Philippians to imitate him and to observe those who take Paul as a model because he himself exemplifies humble-mindedness in his life (3:17 and 4:9). Together with Christ, all Christians share a heavenly citizenship (*politeuma*) which Paul contrasts with the destiny of the 'enemies of the cross' whose 'minds are set on earthly things' (*ta epigeia phronountes*) whose god is the belly (3:18–19). It is this contrasting citizenship of earth and heaven that explains Paul's reference to 'the body of our humiliation' that he says will be transformed by Christ so that it will become like his 'body of glory' (3:21). This is not a denigration of the human body. Indeed 'body' is quite a positive word in Paul, unlike 'flesh' which has a quite different meaning as we shall see. Here Paul suggests that a Christian's final obedience is to Christ and no other, his or her final destiny is heaven and, for this to be brought to fruition, the body of humiliation (*to sōma tēs tapeinōseōs*) must be transformed just as he describes it in 1 Corinthians 15:35–54, where a body that he characterises as perishable, dishonourable, weak, mortal and en-souled (*sōma psuchikon*) [often misleadingly translated as 'physical body'[4]], is to become imperishable, honourable, powerful, immortal and en-Spirited (*sōma pneumatikon*) at the resurrection, just as Christ's was.

This bodily transformation that Paul calls 'resurrection' corresponds to the second strophe of the Philippians hymn:

> Therefore God also highly exalted him and gave him the
>   name that is above every name [i.e., 'Lord'],
> so that at the name of Jesus every knee should bend, in
>   heaven and on earth and under the earth,
> and every tongue should confess that Jesus Christ is Lord, to
>   the glory of God the Father.

Humility, the giving up of status, has its fulfilment in an exaltation in which, Paul believes, one receives everything that is worthwhile. This may be what he is hinting at later in the letter when he says, 'I know what it is to have little, and I know what it is to have plenty', even though the immediate context is his material welfare (4:11–14). He was certainly not talking about material wealth when he wrote of Christ being rich but becoming poor for the sake of those in Corinth 'so that by his poverty you might become rich' (2 Corinthians 8:9). And the same is true when he wrote of his own renunciation of worldly status:

> Yet whatever gains I had, these I have come to regard as loss because of Christ. More than that, I regard everything as loss because of the surpassing value of knowing Christ Jesus my Lord. For his sake I have suffered the loss of all things, and I regard them as rubbish, in order that I may gain Christ and be found in him. (Philippians 3:7–9)

---

4   See ch. 6 n 2. For a full explanation of this see N. T. Wright, *The Resurrection of the Son of God* (London: SPCK, 2003), pp. 348–52.

Paul is throughout playing on paradoxes of richness and poverty, the material and the spiritual, in which the focus is on reversal.[5]

While the theme of humility is at the very centre of Philippians, such a key idea inevitably finds a place in his other letters. The Christians in Corinth are told that 'God chose what is low and despised in the world' (1 Corinthians 1:28), which is just as well for them as not many were born wise or powerful or of noble rank (1:26). They were already of low social and intellectual status, exactly what is meant by *tapeinos*, humble. Their task was to accept it, not cultivate resentment or struggle to better themselves in the world. Even those in other communities who were born to higher status should not think too highly of themselves (Galatians 6:3; Romans 12:3), because God consoles those who are made humble or, perhaps we should say, those who have been humiliated.[6] Paul uses the language of Philippians in Romans 12:16 too (though you would not know it from NRSV) where he tells his readers to have the same mind among themselves, not to think lofty things of themselves but to associate with the humble (or it could mean: condescend to do humble things) and not become high-minded or haughty. In 1 Corinthians Paul castigates his readers for taking each other to court before pagan judges, which he said was already a defeat for them whatever the judgement of the court: 'Why not rather be wronged? Why not rather be defeated?' (1 Corinthians 6:7) – indeed humiliated. It is because humility is so fundamental to the Christian life that Paul himself was prepared, as an apostle, to become a spectacle and a fool to the world (4:9f). This was how he presented himself to those in Corinth – but it does not seem to have had the desired effect (2 Corinthians 10:1f; 11:7).

There is another side to all this. We have to beware of false humility (Colossians 2:23) and any humiliation which is forced on us is not to be welcomed (Colossians 2:18). It is certainly not something to force on your brethren (1 Corinthians 11:22). Humil-

---

5 This discussion has been much influenced by the excellent analysis of Peter Doble, '"Vile Bodies" or Transformed Persons' in *Journal for the Study of the New Testament*, 86, 2002, pp. 3–27.

6 The word is *tapeinos* which NRSV translates as 'the downcast' (2 Cor. 7:6) and 'the lowly' (Rom. 12:16)!

ity is something the Christian has to take upon himself/herself. Humility is a pattern of life to be chosen and accepted willingly. It must involve renunciation of status, maybe even abandoning one's career for a socially less ambitious form of life. More generally it means not making claims to status or privilege, not standing upon one's status or demanding deference. (Bishops take note.) It means giving up control of one's life and placing others first. This is demanding but not as rare as one might think, for it is something which will be familiar to every good parent. But now it is something to be expected of our relationships with everyone.

It is at this point that the Christian narrative, which has Jesus at its centre, runs counter to what society reckons is sensible. The ancient and the modern world alike have at their centre the desire to dethrone God and take power, in effect turning men and women themselves into gods. Greek mythology warns us of Prometheus who snatched fire from the gods and was punished for his presumption by being chained to a rock and having his liver pecked by a raven for evermore. The same moral can be found in Jewish culture in the story of the people of Babel who built an enormous tower to storm the heavens and seize the power that rightly belongs only to God. So God scattered the human race over the face of the earth and made them speak various mutually unintelligible languages to prevent future co-operation. In each case their sin was hubris, pride. The wisdom of the ancient world knew that humankind had to keep its proper place; to overreach oneself is to court disaster.

Far from heeding the ancient warning, there are some modern narratives that still recommend that God be displaced so that humankind can become its own god. Humankind in its pride wishes to be under no one. The obvious example is Sigmund Freud's 'God', the moral superego who takes away our moral freedom. In a theological context, Ludwig Feuerbach at the beginning of the nineteenth century saw 'God' as an illusory projection of what he called the species-being of the human race, that is, he thought of God as a fictional ideal-human who encapsulates all the characteristics of what it would be to be fully human. Feuerbach's god is the idealisation of humankind and to that extent represents a moral ideal of what we might aim for, but for Feuerbach it is an illusory idealisation that has become an obstacle to men and women reaching their destiny as free moral and social beings. God has to go so that humankind can take God's place, not in the heavens but on earth.

Iris Murdoch interpreted Plato's idea of the Good in much the same way.[7] She suggested that the Good did not exist substantially, not even for Plato – it should certainly not be thought to be the moral actualisation of God – but, as an ideal Platonic form, its purpose for Plato is to act as a representation of the moral perfection that we ought to strive for.

Whatever his virtues as a critic of nineteenth-century capitalism, Karl Marx adopted the same view of God as Feuerbach. Marx wrote very little about religion but he took it seriously enough as we can see in the famous passage from his *Critique of Hegel's Philosophy of Right*, where religious obeisance to an illusory God is a reflection of social obeisance to actual human authorities in church and state, and where religious piety is a response, but an alienated response, to real suffering as it was experienced in the world of early Western capitalism. Marx tells us that deference to God distracts people from their social oppression by church and state, and their condition will only begin to change when they throw off the illusory happiness offered by religion to change their material conditions, for they have nothing to lose but their chains. For Marx, 'God' gets in the way of our living a free human life. To believe in God is to be alienated from the true nature of the world. It is to live a lie and to be drawn away from changing the material quality of human life. It is a lie foisted on the poor by the rich to facilitate their exploitation. In effect Marx says that people should stop being humble and take control of their lives. Nietzsche says much the same (and more) as we shall see: kill off God to become human. It is as though modern secular societies are carrying out a moral experiment to discover whether the abandonment of God and traditional religious values will lead to a more human and fulfilling world. So far they have not been conspicuously successful. If moral development could keep pace with technological development all would be well, but human morality cannot be manipulated so easily. As we enter the twenty-

---

7   Iris Murdoch, *The Sovereignty of Good* (London: Routledge, 1970).

first century the fate of the human race is in the balance and may be found wanting. The problem for humanity is sin but what Paul says about this is for a later chapter.

3

Slavery

Slavery in the Ancient World

Friedrich Nietzsche thoroughly despised what he called the slave morality of Christianity. In *Beyond Good and Evil* (1886) and the first part of *The Genealogy of Morals* (1887) he contrasted those ethics that enabled you to become *master* of your life with those – chiefly religious moralities – that, as he saw it, sucked the life out of you and left you as a *slave*, subject to the whims of others and your own worst instincts. The last thing he thought people should be is humble. People ought to take charge of their lives with a 'will to power' so that they could become a superior person (what Nietzsche called an *Übermensch*), someone who would rise above the mass. In particular he had nothing but contempt for a religion that promoted values like humility, kindness, compassion and forgiveness – in other words: Christianity. Nietzsche might not have been a Nazi before its time but it is easy to see how his ideas could have been used to feed the worst excesses of fascism. Rather than looking to the long-dead Führer, I think a closer example of what it might be to be a Nietzschean *Übermensch*, one who takes a grip of their destiny, one who believes in getting on in the world, is Margaret Thatcher – and I do not think she would be entirely insulted by the suggestion.

In claiming that Christianity had a slave morality, Nietzsche was more accurate than he knew, though not in quite the way he thought. To understand this we have to look to Paul's letters where he has something remarkable to say about slavery. A difficulty for many modern readers is that Paul made no overt criticism of the slavery of his day. This has become a particular embarrassment for Christians, black and white, in the United States since the abolition of slavery in the nineteenth century. Paul does not seem to match their model of what it is to be a modern American; in regard to slavery he seems to be too close to rednecks. How can Paul be respected when he seems to have accepted slavery as a given part of the structure of society in the ancient world? For a strict evangelical who wants to follow every word of the New Testament this may imply that slavery could be acceptable in modern society. However, no one in the ancient world ever thought to question slavery, save Gregory of Nyssa (*c.*330–*c.*395), who was the sole Christian exception, and, according to Philo, the Essenes at Qumran. Peter Garnsey writes:

> Gregory of Nyssa's lively attack on slave-owning as an aspect of the sin of pride is unique. Slave-owning, it is clear, was a structural element of Christian as well as pagan and Jewish society and was accepted as such by Church leaders.

In the final sentence of his study of slavery, Garnsey writes: 'It will surprise no one that the hero of my narrative is Gregory of Nyssa who, perhaps uniquely, saw that slavery is a sin.'[1]

Of all the early Church Fathers, only Gregory thought that slave-owning was a sin. Paul didn't; nor did anyone else. Paul, then, is simply representative of his age in accepting slavery as a given. Yet it turns out that he did far more than merely acquiesce in the conventional values of his age.

Philosophical arguments about slavery were not uncommon in the ancient world, especially among Stoic philosophers. Of course, it was an educated and leisured class that wrote philosophy and they were among those who benefited economically from having slaves. So the standard approach was to justify the social and economic status quo by supposing, as Aristotle did for example, that most people were inferior by nature and needed to be guided – as slaves – by wiser men. This was assumed to be for the good of the slaves as well as the slave-masters, as it was thought they would not be able to manage their lives without firm guidance. Slaves were seen as

---

1 P. Garnsey, *Ideas of Slavery from Aristotle to Augustine* (Cambridge: CUP, 1996), pp. 240, 243.

children who would never make it socially to adulthood. This harsh doctrine was ameliorated only by the Stoics who spoke of slavery metaphorically as well as literally, so that they were able to distinguish between literal, chattel slavery of the body and slavery of the mind or spirit. They suggested that slavery of the body was not such a bad thing provided one's human spirit was free, for they supposed that material matters were trivial by comparison with the spiritual. Yet this argument was clearly dishonest, for it ensured that nothing changed. Masters continued to have the benefit of owning slaves – but with a clear philosophical conscience.

Garnsey summarises the Stoic position in this way:

> institutional slavery is beyond our control and not worth bothering about;
> slavery of the mind is within our own control and is worth bothering about;
> only the wise or the good man is free – the foolish or bad man is slavish;
> so the Stoics concluded that as wise men are very few, most men (and *a fortiori* women and children) are inferior and moral-spiritual slaves – and it is appropriate that these people should be chattel slaves too.[2]

This was a fine argument for ensuring that a social elite continued to control and exploit the majority. This argument would have suited Nietzsche, for there is no hint of social equality in his writings. The logic of his position is that society will and should contain slaves but, as an *Übermensch*, he was not going to be one of them. He adopted a master-morality, and where there is a master there are perforce also underlings. Neither the Stoics' nor Nietzsche's argument is one that would have impressed many slaves, but then few of them have ever read philosophy. In contrast to the Stoics, however (and presumably Nietzsche), Garnsey condemns slavery as 'the most degrading and exploitative institution invented by man'.[3]

---

2 Garnsey, *Ideas of Slavery*, p. 133.
3 Garnsey, *Ideas of Slavery*, p. 5.

Every Greek and Roman citizen, including Paul, would have grasped the reality of slavery in a way that we do not. Even though there are still slaves in the world, it is a social reality remote from most of us in the West. But it was not remote for those in the ancient world. Then prisoners of war were commonly used as slaves, rather as Russian prisoners were in the 1940s by Germany, and British prisoners by the Japanese, but ancient Greece and Rome transformed the practice into 'an institutional system of large-scale employment of slave labor in both countryside and the cities'.[4] It has been suggested that Rome's later wars were in effect slave hunts. It is estimated that 30 per cent or more of the population of Roman Italy at the beginning of the Christian era were slaves or freed slaves, though the figure is thought to have been about half this elsewhere in the Empire. These remarkable statistics show that everyone in the ancient world knew what slavery was like either because they owned slaves or because they were slaves – often being born into slavery – or were freed slaves, or at least they knew slaves. Slaves were to be seen everywhere.

In recent years we have been offered contradictory pictures of what the experience of slavery was like. Until fairly recently scholars of the period suggested that the experience of being a slave might not have been too bad. It is known that slaves were allowed to save money with which they might buy their freedom and then perhaps start a business, maybe with their former master. It was possible for some slaves to work in skilled trades or be given responsibility as household or financial managers. They might also have acted as a tutor or governess (*paidogōgos*) to the master's children. Slaves could have expected to be freed by the age of thirty – if they reached that age – though this prospect had been designed to head off mass revolts as it discouraged slaves from running away, the penalty for which would have been severe if they were caught. Better to stay on as a slave and hope for eventual freedom. Freed slaves were often awarded Roman citizenship – something the Greeks found extraordinary – and occasionally one might rise high in society like the

---

4 M. I. Finley, *Ancient Slavery and Modern Ideology*, (New York: Viking Press, 1980), p. 67.

Roman governor Marcus Antonius Felix mentioned in Acts 23—24. At the least slavery would offer food and a roof over one's head and sometimes those overwhelmed by debt would voluntarily sell themselves into slavery, though that would have been a desperate thing to do and was always a last resort.

In the last couple of decades we have come to realise that slavery was not as benign as that. Roman state law tends to give an idealised picture of how slaves should be treated and scholars of the ancient world now put more emphasis on sociological evidence, such as inscriptions, to find out what really went on. While it was long thought that slaves were guaranteed their freedom by thirty years of age, other evidence suggests that the decree was that slaves should not be freed *before* they reached thirty, but as average mortality at that time was about thirty years for the whole population, slaves would be worn out by that age and literally past their sell-by date. A slave's life expectancy would have been less than thirty, so it is likely that only a limited number of slaves would have lived long enough to be freed.[5] Most manumitted slaves gained their freedom at the death of their masters, who often provided for it in their wills. No, the other side of the coin is that someone taken into slavery became a non-person without any legal rights, was often treated brutally and could be killed almost with impunity. They could not marry, hold property or give evidence in court.[6] The penalties for running away were severe and they would be crucified if involved in a rebellion. Jane Glancy has shown how slaves, particularly women slaves, were the sexual chattels of their owners.[7] Most slaves in Italy seem to have worked as unpaid farm workers on the rural estates of their masters. Bizarrely, these landowners often came by their estates by confiscating land from peasants who were unable pay their debts because they had been conscripted into the army and stationed abroad

---

5   R. A. Horsley, 'The Slave Systems of Classical Antiquity and their Reluctant Recognition by Modern Scholars', *Semeia*, 83/84 (1998), pp. 48ff.

6   C. Hezser, 'Slaves and Slavery in Rabbinic and Roman Law' in *Rabbinic Law in its Roman and Near Eastern Context*, ed. C. Hezser (Tübingen: Mohr Siebeck, 2003), pp. 133–76.

7   J. A. Glancy, *Slavery in Early Christianity* (Oxford: OUP, 2002).

where they could not pay their rents. Some slaves ran away and succeeded in 'disappearing' but most stayed with their owners out of fear.

Slavery was less common in the Middle East where the land was worked by serfs in hock to landlords rather than slaves as such. The Jews had their own laws which made it less likely that they would enslave fellow Jews. Jewish slaves of a Jewish master had (in principle) to be released within seven years. Circumcised Gentile slaves in effect became members of their household, where they worked as domestic servants on a par with natural-born Jews. So when the Bible speaks of slaves it is often difficult to know whether it refers to the harsh slavery of the Romans or to domestic service. Because of these regulations which were peculiar to Judaism, Paul may not have seen slavery everywhere in Israel, but when he wrote to the churches of Greece, Asia Minor and Italy, he was writing to communities that included slaves and manumitted slaves. He knew the reality they had to endure and, of course, he knew of slavery as a foundational experience of his own people at the Exodus. This makes what Paul does with the language of slavery all the more remarkable.

Paul and Chattel Slavery

In some of his letters, notably at the end of Romans, Paul names various individuals and some of them, it is thought, might well have been freed slaves. The Letter to Philemon is addressed to one particular Christian slave-master who is asked to take back his slave Onesimus and treat him compassionately. Onesimus had been supporting Paul while he had been in prison (someone had to bring food to a prisoner because the guards would not do it) and the traditional understanding is that Onesimus was a slave who had taken Paul's message of Christian freedom literally and run away, but whom Paul was now sending back to his master. Some now doubt whether Onesimus ever had been a slave, though verses 15–16 of the letter suggest he was. The point is that Philemon is urged to receive Onesimus as a Christian brother.

There is nothing to threaten social revolution in this short letter, nor in the advice on relations between masters and Christian slaves given in the next generation of pseudo-Pauline letters, written in the latter part of the first century. There is no hint in Colossians (which might be by Paul) nor in Ephesians (which is probably not by Paul) that slavery might be unacceptable:

> Slaves, obey your earthly masters in everything, not only while being watched and in order to please them, but wholeheartedly, fearing the Lord. Whatever your task, put yourselves into it, as done for the Lord and not for your masters, since you know that from the Lord you will receive the inheritance as your reward; you serve the Lord Christ. (Colossians 3:22–24)

Then, on the principle of reciprocity, the author adds: 'Masters, treat your slaves justly and fairly, for you know that you also have a Master in heaven' (Colossians 4:1; and see also Ephesians 6:5–9 which looks derivative of Colossians). Whether this comes from Paul or not, it meshes well with the advice Paul gives on being a good citizen:

> Let every person be subject to the governing authorities ... those authorities that exist have been instituted by God ... It [the state] is the servant of God to execute wrath on the wrongdoer. Therefore one must be subject, not only because of wrath but also because of conscience ... Pay to all what is due to them – taxes ... revenue ... respect ... honour. (Romans 13:1–7)

Because of his acceptance of social realities such as slavery, Paul has often been criticised for being subservient to the state but if in this he is guilty, so is everyone else in the early Christian era, pagan, Jew and Christian, with that one notable exception in the fourth century, Gregory of Nyssa. No one in the first century thought that slavery would or could or should be abolished. It was virtually unthinkable. The stability of society demanded a body of slaves, and social stability was essential when you consider how the Pax Romana was threatened by the wild tribes outside the Empire to the north.

'Slavery' as a Metaphor

Paul begins to get interesting on this subject when he starts to talk about slavery metaphorically. The nature of his argument demands that we look carefully at the detail of what he has written. He sets the tone in Galatians 2:4 where he complains about false brothers secretly brought into the local church in Antioch to 'enslave us'. These men were baptised Pharisees like himself who had come to Antioch from Jerusalem to press Gentile converts to obey the Torah, specifically on circumcision. Here Paul clearly regards slavery as a bad thing, reflecting the social reality of enslavement in the Roman Empire, and it is this reality that feeds his negative use of the metaphor in the central passages of Galatians 4 and Romans 6—7.

In this metaphor, what is it that we are enslaved to? Paul's first suggestion is that it is 'the elemental spirits of the world' (*ta stoicheia tou kosmou*, Galatians 4:1). He says it is 'we' who are enslaved, and behind this lies a narrative that 'we' are involved in. Paul also says that minors, before they reach the age of legal adulthood, have no more rights than slaves. They remain under a legal guardian – the *paidagōgos* of Galatians 3:24 and 25 – until a date to be set by the father. In this image, Paul speaks in parallel both of slaves becoming free and children reaching adulthood, in which the master of the slave is the 'elemental spirits' and the guardian of the child is 'the law' (3:24). Paul runs these two images in parallel in Galatians when he says that we have been both enslaved to the elemental spirits and yoked to the law. 'We', then, have been both slaves and children, at one and the same time subjected both to the elemental spirits and to the law. However, Paul's main point is that the father's appointed date has now come. We were minors who have now become adult heirs *and* we were slaves who have been adopted and so brought into the family as children to become heirs. The double image might at first be confusing but no doubt Paul used it for emphasis. We can see Paul merging the two images when he writes, 'So you are no longer a slave but a child, and if a child then also an heir, through God' (4:7).

When he wrote of children and slaves, it is possible that Paul may have been thinking about the place of Jews and Gentiles in the church but, if so, he has not been clear in differentiating them. At any rate, the power of the elemental spirits and the authority of the law over us have ended. We are adults and free citizens.

There is another associated issue here. Who exactly is Paul's 'we' of Galatians 4? Is it equivalent to the 'I' of Romans 7:7–25? There is no general agreement among critics about the identity of the 'I' in Romans 7 but, as with Galatians 4, there is an implied narrative behind the text for that 'I'. The passage tells us that sin has been in the world [from the time of Adam] but 'I' did not know sin until it was brought to life by the law [from the time of Moses]. The law is holy and just and good because it has come from God, but it aroused all kinds of sinfulness (Paul's particular example is covetousness) 'in me' and 'I' died. 'For sin, seizing an opportunity in the commandment, deceived me and through it killed me' (7:12). Paul can also write, 'I was once alive apart from the law, but when the commandment came, sin revived and I died' (7:9). Yet at no time was Paul himself actually alive apart from the law, so he cannot be writing about himself. He is not himself the 'I' of Romans 7. What he has in fact done is to outline the history of the Jewish people from Adam/sin to Moses/law and to the present time, which has been a time of spiritual death. So 'I' seems to represent the Jewish people, of whom Paul is a member.

It is sin, however, which is at the root of the problem not the law (7:7–12). Paul speaks about sin from verse 14 as it affects not just Jews but the whole human race. Paul is not being autobiographical here, he is writing about the history and spiritual experience of the human race but from the standpoint of a Christ-believing Jew. All the same, the experience of emotional conflict and moral inadequacy expressed in 7:15–20 includes Paul, for it certainly sounds as though Paul knew what it was to covet and, because of the Ten Commandments, he knew it was wrong. So the 'we' of Galatians 4 (the earlier letter) and the 'I' of Romans 7 are intimately related. Both passages are about the whole human race but observed from a Jewish point of view – and both are related to the idea of slavery.

If we return to Galatians 4, we find that Paul continues to identify our slave-master as the elemental spirits (*stoicheia*) who 'by nature are not gods' (Galatians 4:8–9). But when Paul returns to the theme of slavery at v. 21, the slave-master is now the law. At this point he moves into his famous allegory in which he relates the slave-woman

Hagar to her and Abraham's son Ishmael (who is not actually named here), to flesh, to the Sinai covenant (law), and to the present Jerusalem whose inhabitants are 'children of slavery'. He contrasts this series with Abraham's other son Isaac, his mother Sarah, promise, the Jerusalem above and freedom. And he adds that 'she [Sarah] is our mother', i.e., not Hagar (4:26). Paul's outrageous implication is that his contemporary synagogue-Jews are descended from Hagar and Ishmael, and his fellow Christ-believing Jews are, together with adopted and baptised Gentiles, the true spiritual descendants of Sarah and Isaac. He tells this latter group that they are children of the promise (to Abraham) who must 'not submit again to the yoke of slavery' (5:1). So Paul implies that his Christian readers in Galatia have been freed from a form of slavery that was slavery to the elemental spirits *and* to the law which had come from Sinai, i.e., the Torah. It is worth pointing out, however, that Paul's is not an anti-Jewish argument; it is an argument, strained though it might seem, about who is the true Israel, the true descendants of Abraham. And Paul concludes that it is not those who keep Torah, but those who are obedient to Jesus Christ, the Messiah.

When we move to Romans 6—7, we find that Paul shifts the metaphor from slavery to elemental spirits and/or law to one of a slavery to sin. Here Paul develops a number of further associations, where being a slave to sin leads to impurity, iniquity, shame and death:

> Do you not know that if you present yourselves to anyone as obedient slaves, you are slaves to the one whom you obey, either of sin, which leads to *death* ...
>
> You once presented your members as slaves to *impurity* and to greater and greater *iniquity* ...
>
> When you were slaves to sin, you were free in regard to righteousness. So what advantage did you then get from the things of which you now are *ashamed*? The end of those things is *death*.
>
> ... the wages of sin is *death*. (6:16, 19, 20, 21, 23)

In this very Jewish argument, to be freed from the captivity of sin and all its consequences, there must be a death. We have to die to sin and this death takes place in baptism. Of course, it is a metaphorical death – there is no death by drowning here – but it is still a real death for one's old self and it leads to 'newness of life' or a new life (6:3–7).

In chapter 7 Paul shifts his imagery yet again and speaks of dying to the law. This implies that he and his readers had been enslaved to the law – precisely the language he had used in Galatians, as we have seen:

> you have died to the law through the body of Christ ... now we are discharged from the law, dead to that which held us captive, so that we are slaves not under the old written code but in the new life of the spirit [or Spirit]. (7:4, 6)

It is in this passage that the three central forms of the oppression of humanity at last appear together in Paul's argument: sin, law and death; with 'flesh' used to characterise the state of humanity before baptism and spiritual liberation. 'While we were living in the flesh, our sinful passions, aroused by the law, were at work in our members to bear fruit for death' (7:5). So while his readers may once have been slaves to sin and the rest, Paul tells them that they have now received a spirit of adoption which has made them children and heirs so that they might not 'fall back into fear' (8:15). Finally he applies the metaphor of slavery to the whole of creation which has been 'subjected to futility' in a 'bondage of decay', which groans in pain, waiting for the revealing of the sons (NRSV: children) of God (8:19–22).

Paul's Transformation of 'Slavery'

Throughout the whole of this Paul has spoken of slavery in a purely negative sense. Slavery is something we need to escape from. Given the nature of chattel slavery in Paul's own society, this is what you would expect, even though he is not actually speaking about chattel slavery at this point but slavery to sin with its associations to flesh, law, impurity, iniquity and death. However, in the middle of all this Paul does something extraordinary. He begins to speak of slavery in a positive way, albeit still metaphorically.

Paul makes this important move in Romans. In Galatians all the positive talk is about redemption and adoption, while slavery stays entirely negative: 'So you are no longer a slave ... stand firm and do not submit again to a yoke of slavery' (Galatians 4:7; 5:1).

In Romans, however, he finds a new way of talking about slavery, so that slavery becomes for Paul an integral part of the pattern of Christian life. Now he presents us with a contrast between a slavery to sin on the one hand and on the other a slavery of obedience to God and to righteousness and to 'the form of teaching to which you were entrusted' (Romans 6:16–17). The Christians in Rome are told that they should present themselves 'as slaves to righteousness for sanctification' (6:19). 'But now that you have been freed from sin and enslaved to God, the advantage you get is sanctification, and the end/goal (*telos*) is eternal life' (6:22).

This shift in Paul's language from the negative to the positive is rarely remarked on, yet he now invites his readers to think about slavery in a new way. Paul subverts traditional ways of thinking about slavery simply as a form of oppression. Paul's challenge to his readers is to understand slavery positively without at the same time approving chattel slavery. He comes to think that being a slave is, in some form, an ineluctable part of being human. In Paul's existential sense, this is just as true for slave-masters as for slaves, even though it is the masters who think they are free because they enjoy the material benefits of chattel slavery. In Paul's scheme, all unbelievers, all the unbaptised, are slaves to sin and are under the control of the *stoicheia*, the elemental spirits of the world, while the baptised are slaves to righteousness. Paul implies that everyone owes obedience to something or someone. Yet obedience can be good or bad depending on what or who it is you obey.

> Do you not know that if you present yourselves to anyone as obedient slaves, you are slaves of the one whom you obey, either of sin, which leads to death, or of obedience, which leads to righteousness? But thanks be to God that you, having once been slaves of sin, have become obedient from the heart to the form of teaching to which you were entrusted, and that you, having been set free from sin, have become slaves of righteousness. (6:16–18)

So there seem to be two forms of slavery and we have to choose which master to obey: either the axis of sin, law, impurity and death, characterised as life in the flesh; or God who brings righteousness, sanctification and eternal life, which Paul characterises as life in the spirit. Theologically, slavery is no longer unequivocally oppressive. Paul tells his readers that, paradoxically, there is a form of slavery that brings freedom, the freedom to do what we truly desire (7:14–24), the freedom not to be condemned (8:1). This is very different from the slave morality castigated by Nietzsche.

All this allows Paul to speak of himself and his fellow believers as 'slaves of Jesus Christ' (Philippians 1:1; Galatians 1:10 and Romans 1:1, though English translations often soften this to 'servants'). Paul has in turn become a slave to those in the church in Corinth (2 Corinthians 4:5) and Christians in their turn must 'through love become slaves to one another' (Galatians 5:13). This is a slavery that brings equality to all who submit to it. It is Paul's 'obedience of faith'. Paul even says that he has made himself a slave to *everyone* so that he might win more of them to the gospel (1 Corinthians 9:19), and this introduces a highly rhetorical passage in which he shows that he would not put any social or racial barrier in the way of winning converts (9:19–23).

The foundation for this positive understanding of what it might be to be a slave is christological. The best expression is in Philippians 2:5–11, which, as we have seen, is carefully structured, in two strophes of three lines each, and of a style that suggests it was used in Christian worship. In this passage we are told that Christ Jesus was in the form of God (*en morphē theou*) but lowered/emptied himself to take the form of a slave (*morphēn doulou labōn*), born in human likeness. This last line does indeed suggest that being human entails being a slave of some sort. That is what Jesus became when he became human. For him, becoming a slave brought obedience, humility and death. However, death on a cross leads in the second strophe of the Philippians poem to exaltation. Christ gave up everything to receive everything. For a Christian, then, becoming a slave means identifying 'with Christ' and living 'in Christ' to use Paul's own expressions. It means, to follow the language of Philippians, having the same mind as Christ and Paul and one another, which is humble-mindedness.

Slavery in the Christian Life

What does this mean in practice? We have already seen that it essentially involves not seeking or claiming social status. In Philippians 2 it also means doing nothing from selfish ambition or conceit, sharing the same love, regarding others as better than yourselves, not looking to your own interests but to those of others, not murmuring or arguing, remaining blameless and guiltless, being 'children of God without blemish in the midst of a crooked and perverse generation, in which you shine like stars in the world' (2:15).

Paul contrasts this with the mindedness of those who are set on earthly things, 'enemies of the cross of Christ' whose end is shame and destruction (3:18–19). The humble-minded, on the other hand, have their citizenship in the heavenly places.

Surprising as Paul's language might seem, he was only developing a theme that came in the first place from Jesus and can be found in the Gospels. We have to take the lower place at table and wait to be called up, for the first will be last and last first (Mark 10:31). Jesus criticised the Pharisees' love of taking the seats of honour in the synagogues and seeking signs of respect in the marketplace (Luke 11:43). And when he observed how guests behaved at a banquet, coveting the places of honour, he told his disciples, 'all who exalt themselves will be humbled and those who humble themselves will be exalted' (Luke 14:11) – this is presumably an eschatological promise, something stored up for the future. Jesus also said that while Gentile rulers lord it over their citizens, 'it is not so among you; but whoever wishes to become great among you must be your servant, and whoever wishes to be first among you must be slave of all' (Mark 10:43). In church tradition, the model for this – after Jesus – has been Mary. In Luke's hymn, God has looked with favour on 'the lowliness of his servant', or literally 'the humility/humiliation of his slave girl' (*tēn tapeinōsin tēs doulēs autou*, Luke 1:48). She was humiliated by becoming pregnant at her age in her social position, but God looks on her with favour.

Slavery, then, is of the essence of the Christian life, provided one understands it in Paul's sense. For Paul, being a slave is metaphorical, theological but real. The refusal to search for status should frame the whole pattern of one's behaviour towards others. If ever there was a transvaluation of all values, to use Nietzsche's expression, this is it. It makes Nietzsche's attempt to overthrow traditional Christian values look mean and dangerous, a sordid trampling underfoot of those who do not share the advantages of his super-people, who these days are sometimes called, non-ironically I believe, 'the beautiful people' (*Übermenschen*).

Of course, Paul did not go far enough. It could be argued that his argument is compatible with that of Aristotle or the Stoics, which was to free the mind and regard bodily troubles as trivial, while social structures remained unchanged. Paul certainly shifted the ground for talking about slavery – if anyone had ever understood what he was up to – but we had to wait many centuries before a serious move was made to abolish chattel slavery. Paul's shift was to see everyone as being a slave: the unbaptised (whether master or slave) are slaves of sin, while the baptised (whether master or chattel slave) are slaves of righteousness.

There may be a further reason for Paul having used the image of the slave to illustrate the Christian life. The good slave is obedient to a master and should be a model of fidelity. Fidelity is also at the heart of Paul's theology as we find it in Galatians and Romans.

4

Faithfulness I

There is no question that 'faith' is central to Paul's thinking. It is the crucial element in that brief phrase that is familiar to all who have read anything by or about Paul: justification by faith. Since at least the beginning of the sixteenth century this has been thought to be the leading motif in Paul (and some would say in the whole of Christian theology) even though the expression only occurs in Romans, Galatians and briefly in Philippians. It is so important theologically that it has been thought to control every other idea, not only in Paul's letters but in theology generally. This is a very Protestant approach and derives from Martin Luther who believed that salvation is from faith alone: *sola fide*. Yet this phrase has been a mark of division since the Reformation, as the Roman Catholic Church, echoing the Letter of James in the New Testament, has stood by 'faith and works'. However, formal agreement between the Lutheran and Catholic Churches was reached in 1999 in this area and, while not all points of disagreement and emphasis have been resolved, both can agree that the motif means that salvation is by grace alone.[1] It comes from God, not human striving.

Paradoxically, just at the time this agreement was being forged, many Protestant scholars were reassessing the place of justification by faith in Paul's thought and were daring to say that Luther had got

---

1 The *Joint Declaration on the Doctrine of Justification* by The Lutheran World Federation and the Roman Catholic Church, ratified in Augsburg on 31 October 1999 (Reformation Day!), can be easily found on the internet. There is a useful discussion of this short document edited by David Aune, *Reading Paul Together: Protestant and Catholic Perspectives on Justification* (Grand Rapids, MI: Baker Academic, 2006).

it wrong. It was now being suggested that it was not the case that Paul promoted a Christian life in which good works had no relation to salvation. Nor should justification by faith be placed at the centre of Paul's theology. Some earlier writers like Albert Schweitzer (1875–1965) had tried to move justification away from the centre and replace it, in his case, with what he called Paul's 'mysticism', an interpretation of Paul which centred on his frequent use of the expression 'in Christ' (*The Mysticism of Paul the Apostle*, 1930/1). By the 1980s critics like Ed Sanders, Tom Wright and James Dunn were saying that Luther's interpretation was actually a misreading of Paul. Luther's understanding, it would seem, had been skewed by his own circumstances as an Augustinian friar, disillusioned by the devotional practices he had observed in Rome and disgusted by the selling of indulgences in Germany, plagued by moral scruples in his monastery and fretting over how he – a sinner – could stand uncondemned before God. When he had to deliver a set of lectures on Romans in 1515–16 Luther discovered Paul's assertion that we are justified by our faith in Jesus (Romans 3:26b) and he thought it was the answer to his theological problems, which at the same time were also personal problems. Consequently Luther adopted a very individualistic understanding of justification by faith and thought it was primarily about the relationship of the individual to God, the judge before whom all had to stand in the dock. He also thought that it was about the impossibility of any good coming from human actions, implying the wrong-headedness of attaching the idea of merit to religious and moral behaviour. It was about the power of God's grace, which Luther thought was literally irresistible once (and if) anyone received it. Luther had a famous exchange at about this time with Erasmus over whether a person has the free will to rebel against God's grace. Erasmus thought you could (the Catholic position) even though it would be foolish, indeed wicked, to do so, while Luther thought a person had free will but not the power to resist because of the overwhelming power of God's grace. In this debate Erasmus was able to attribute wickedness and damnation to human choice, while Luther had to conclude that some people were wicked and damned because God had chosen to withhold his grace from them.

What can be agreed is that justification by faith is a major Pauline idea; it plays an important role in Paul's two grandest theological letters. It is an idea that functions in a particular context: the controversy in the early church about, not *whether* Gentiles could be admitted into the church, but *on what terms* they should be admitted.

Describing the context like that may make the church sound like a social or a sports club framing its rules of admission. In the case of a club, one might ask whether it should accept women as members, or black people, or Jews. Early last century many clubs would not have accepted any of them, though they might have preferred not to make their policy public – a nod and a wink would have been enough. But the church is not a social club and could never have imposed such exclusivity. The church from the beginning could never have refused Jews because it *was* a Jewish group. It saw itself as Israel, the true Israel, albeit founded on a new covenant with a new mediator, Jesus Christ (Hebrews 8:6). For the first Christians to think of themselves as 'the new Israel' was the epitome of Jewish-ness. The issue for the church in the 40s AD was how could *Gentiles* be admitted? Even the synagogue had decreed that they could, provided they became Jewish by accepting Torah. That meant that Gentile men had to be circumcised. In the context of this debate, Paul came to see the Torah as a problem. It might have been given to Moses by God but it had now become a barrier to universal salvation because only the Jews had the Torah. The Gentiles were barred from the privileges of being Jewish unless they un-gentiled themselves, so to speak. The new issue was whether non-Jews could join the messianic-Jewish church while still remaining Gentiles. Essentially this meant remaining uncircumcised.

Paul's Use of the Old Testament

The background to this issue – how one becomes and remains a member of God's people – had already been debated in the Old Testament, not least in the Book of Psalms, under the concept of righteousness. It is significant that the issue can be located in the Psalms because Paul's most mature discussion of justification and righteousness is in Romans, and in Romans Paul quotes extensively from the Jewish Bible, and particularly from Isaiah and Psalms.

First let us take note of a few facts. A standard catalogue of these quotations has been made by Earle Ellis who lists eighty-nine Old Testament quotations in Paul's letters (plus six in Ephesians and the Pastoral Letters).[2] Fifty-three of these can be found in Romans. Of these, thirteen are from the Psalms but, as Ellis counts only those that are explicitly set out as quotations (e.g., 'as it is written'), that number can be increased to twenty-four if we look for matching words. There are only seven other quotations from Psalms in the rest of Paul's letters, according to Ellis's list, and within Romans only Isaiah has more citations. Clearly there is a close relationship between the Psalms and the arguments we find in Romans. We might note in passing that other writers adopt a wider definition than Ellis of what counts as a citation, a definition that is more in tune with writing in the ancient world, and we are now able to see that there are far more citations from and allusions to scripture in Paul's letters than can be found in Ellis's list.

It looks as though Paul knew the content of the Jewish Bible extremely well and had learnt great chunks of it by heart. The Bible that he knew and used was a version of the Greek translation known as the Septuagint (LXX), not the original Hebrew. Richard Hays, a pioneer in this field, has written:

> The vocabulary and cadence of scripture – particularly the LXX – are imprinted deeply on Paul's mind ... His practice of citation shows that he was acquainted with virtually the whole body of texts that were later acknowledged as canonical within Judaism.[3]

Paul's familiarity with the Psalms is hardly surprising as they formed the backbone of Jewish worship, just as the Psalter has done subsequently in much Christian worship such as the daily monastic office. Paul must have often meditated on the meaning and implications of these texts. In practice he does not really use scriptural

---

2 E. E. Ellis, *Paul's Use of the Old Testament* (Edinburgh: Oliver & Boyd, 1957), pp. 150–2.

3 R. B. Hays, *Echoes of Scripture in the Letters of Paul* (New Haven, CT and London: Yale University Press, 1989), pp. 16 and 30.

quotations to prove his arguments, so much as to provide illustrations of how he reads scripture in the light of his new understanding of God and God's plan for the world's salvation that he has discovered through his conversion to Christ. He now sees things in scripture that he had not seen before. Although it must be admitted that he uses scripture in a free and often surprising way that we modern readers might not always be comfortable with.

In the study of Romans, it is universally accepted that Paul's language of justification is forensic and had its origin in the law courts. The language is indeed forensic, but in Paul's case it is more likely to have been derived from scripture, so that the law that lies in the background is the Torah rather than Roman law. Psalm 119 certainly regards the law as a juridical code and we do not need to turn to the secular courts for the background to Paul's thinking about justice and justification. To the contrary, Francis Watson has recently gone so far as to suggest that Paul's doctrine of justification by faith is best understood as an exercise in scriptural interpretation.[4] There may in fact be more to Paul's theology than scriptural exegesis, but the Psalms do actually contain all the words/concepts – and in Greek – that Paul needed to develop his theme in Romans and Galatians: righteousness/justification, faith/faithfulness/trust, sin, wrath, law, redemption. Paul did not have to look outside the Psalms to find his vocabulary and set his mental framework for thinking about justification. Ellis moves towards this conclusion when he says, 'It was only natural that Paul, retaining in his mind Hebrew concepts and thought-forms, should frame his Greek on the analogy of the existing theological vocabulary of the LXX.'[5] But Ellis's interest is in Paul and the Septuagint generally, whereas our interest here is more specifically with justification and the Psalms. It is this connection that we need to explore in order to understand what Paul means by 'justification by faith'.

The Doctrine of Righteousness in the Psalms

The key word in Greek is *dikaiosunē*. This is awkward to translate into English and, depending on context, is sometimes rendered as

---

4 F. Watson, *Paul and Hermeneutics of Faith* (London: T&T Clark International, 2004), p. 53.

5 Ellis, *Paul's Use*, p. 13.

'righteousness' and sometimes as 'justification'. The former is an abstraction but is something that belongs to those who are righteous: namely to God and certain select people – but not everyone. The latter, justification, is a process whereby one becomes just (or righteous) or is pronounced to be a just (or righteous) person. Where the context is specifically forensic, it might be best to translate *dikaios* (righteous, just) as 'innocent', which would indicate someone not deserving of condemnation by the (divine) court. *Dikaiosunē* occurs throughout the Greek version of the Psalms and on most occasions is best translated as 'righteousness'. But it is important to remember that, whether it appears as righteous/righteousness or just/justification, it is one single concept for Paul.

So what do the Psalms have to say about righteousness? The priority of the Psalmist is to affirm the righteousness of God: 'For the Lord is righteous and loves righteousness' (Psalm 10:8/11:7 and Psalms 128/129:4; 144/145:17).[6] As a judge, God is righteous: 'he will judge the world with righteousness, and the people in uprightness' (97/98:9). Sometimes the context is explicitly forensic: 'Judge me, Lord, according to your righteousness, O Lord my God, and let them not rejoice against me' (34/35:24). Righteousness is partly a matter of status: God is righteous *because* he is the judge over the world, regardless of the nature of his judgements (49/50:6), but elsewhere his *character* as a just judge emerges when righteousness is linked with other qualities: mercy (114/116:5), love (145/146:8), and truth (83/84:11; 88/89 *passim*) and most notably in 84/85:10–13:

Mercy and truth are met together,
   righteousness and peace have kissed each other.
Truth has sprung out of the earth,

---

6 The Psalms are numbered slightly differently in the Greek OT (known as the Septuagint or LXX) and the Hebrew (the Masoretic Text or MT). Both numbers have been given here (with the LXX, the lower number, coming first) because, while most readers would follow the Hebrew version in a modern translation such as NRSV, Paul was actually using the Greek. The translation of extracts from the Psalms here reflects the Greek OT that Paul used and is not always the same as NRSV.

and righteousness has looked down from heaven.
For the Lord will give goodness,
   and our land shall yield her fruit.
Righteousness shall go before him,
   and shall set his steps in the way.

This righteousness will endure for ever (111/112:3, 7, 9). Psalm 110/111 is a meditation on several aspects of God's righteousness. This psalm relates it to the covenant, at the centre of which is the election of Israel as a people destined to become righteous, first by virtue of the status that comes from election and then by displaying the moral characteristics of God's own righteousness. Because of this, righteousness is devolved first to the king (71/72) then to the priests (131/132:9) and finally to the whole people.

In Romans 3:20 (and Galatians 2:16) Paul quotes Psalm 142/143:2 to support the view that no one can be regarded as righteous in God's sight. But that is not the general tenor of the Psalms. The one who will dwell with God is,

He who walks blamelessly and performs righteousness,
   who speaks truth in his heart.
Who has not spoken craftily with his tongue,
   nor has done evil to his neighbour,
   nor taken up a reproach against those who dwell nearest to
   him …
He has not lent his money as usury,
   and has not received bribes against the innocent.
   (14/15:2–5)

The Lord will recompense the one who behaves righteously (17/18:20, 24). Of course Paul would argue that no one can reach those standards in practice, but both he and the Psalmist would agree that

The salvation of the righteous is from the Lord,
   and he is their defender in the time of affliction.
The Lord will help them and deliver them,
   and he will rescue them from sinners,

and save them because they have trusted [*elpisan*, literally 'hoped'] in him. (36/37:39f)

Dikaiosunē is without doubt a central theme of the Psalms but the dominant issue surrounding it there is whether God will prove his own righteousness by vindicating his righteous ones in times of persecution and suffering. It is not obvious at first sight that God does vindicate them. To outward appearances they are victims; they seem to have been abandoned. The Psalmist raises the question, 'How long O Lord; will you turn away for ever?' (88/89:46). His prayer is 'In your righteousness deliver me and rescue me, incline your ear to me and save me' (70/71:2). His accusation is 'Those who render me evil for good are my adversaries, because I follow after good [righteousness]' (37/38:20). His plea is 'Wake up! Bestir yourself for my defence, for my cause, my God and my Lord! Vindicate me O Lord, my God, according to your righteousness ... and do not let them rejoice over me' (34/35:23f). Repeatedly the Psalmist asks for God's mercy (50/51) and, because he places his trust in God, he is confident of his eventual vindication. The basis for his hope lies in God's previous action in history and, in Psalms 77/78, 104/105, and 105/106 in particular, the Psalmist summarises the 'grand narrative' of God's action that underpins Jewish history from Abraham to the settlement in the land by way of Isaac, Jacob, Joseph, Moses, Aaron, the exodus and the wilderness experience.

The subsequent confidence of the Psalmist in God's eventual vindication also brings with it the idea that those sinners who have been persecuting him will be destroyed:

> The righteous will rejoice when they see vengeance done;
> they will bathe their feet in the blood of the wicked.
> People will say, 'Surely there is a reward for the righteous,
> surely there is a God who judges on earth'. (57/58:10f)

Psalm 93/94 shows that the Psalmist has no sympathy for the fate of the sinner who has 'killed the widow and fatherless, and murdered the stranger'. This leads us to the concept of God's wrath (*orgē*) against sinners, the unrighteous, which is a preoccupation of

Romans 1—2, though words other than *orgē* (mainly *thumos*) are often used in the Septuagint Psalms for this concept. The unrighteous are usually identified in the Psalms as Gentiles but they can be Israelites too:

> a fire was kindled against Jacob, his anger mounted against Israel.
> Because they had no faith in God and did not trust his saving power.(77/78:21–22)

However, lest it be thought that the Psalmist knows only of a wrathful God, it should be pointed out that he often tempers his language of wrath with that of mercy, as in 102/103:6–14:

> The Lord works vindication and justice for all who are oppressed.
> He has made known his ways to Moses,
>   his acts to the people of Israel.
> The Lord is merciful and gracious,
>   slow to anger and abounding in steadfast love.
> He will not always accuse;
>   nor will he keep his anger for ever.
> He does not dealt with us according to our sins,
>   nor repay us according to our iniquities.
> For as heavens are high above the earth,
>   so great is his steadfast love to those who fear him;
>   as far as the East is from the West,
>   so far he removes our transgressions from us.
> As a father has compassion for his children,
>   So the Lord has compassion for those who fear him.
> For he knows how we are made,
>   he remembers that we are dust.

How are we to gain God's mercy and avoid the wrath that is the fate of the unrighteous? In other words, how do we become righteous in God's eyes? The answer of Psalms is: through *faithfulness*. That means faithfulness to God, and to be faithful to God you have to be in the covenant and stay in it. Being a member of the covenant-community gives you a certain status before God, which is a necessary precondition of being righteous. For the Psalmist, you have to be a Jew, a member of the covenant-community, to be counted righteous. In the first place, then, it is not a moral issue but one of election, which in practice is a matter of birth. According to the Psalms there are two marks of faithfulness to that covenant, which are to avoid idolatry and to keep God's law. This is a matter of observance. For his part, God shows *his* faithfulness by maintaining the covenant from his side: the Israelites might have been punished on occasion, but 'for their sake he remembered his covenant' (105/106:45) and saved them.

A person's righteousness, then, is shown by remaining faithful to the God of the covenant, the God of Abraham, Isaac and Jacob, and keeping clear of idolatry (80/81:8ff; 81/82). The example given to illustrate this in the Psalms is that true Israelite hero, Phinehas (105/106:30f, echoing Numbers 25), who ran an unnamed Israelite and his Midianite woman through with his spear for idolatry and it was 'reckoned to him as righteousness' – exactly the words used in the Septuagint of Abraham for his fidelity to God (Genesis 15:6) and cited by Paul in Romans 4:3. So Paul found the words 'it was reckoned to him as righteousness' in the Psalms as well as in Genesis, but in his letter to Rome he preferred to use the more salubrious example of Abraham with his trust in God's promises than the viciousness of Phineas, though both had proved their faithfulness to God's covenant.

So God is righteous and remains faithful to his promises; the Israelites are counted righteous by virtue of their inclusion in the covenant and remain righteous by sticking faithfully with the God of the covenant and no other. Forensic language is normally used in the Psalms (and elsewhere) to account for God preserving the status of the Israelites when he judges in favour of his righteous ones (*dikaioi*).

But now a note on the language of Paul and the Septuagint Psalms. Paul, we may suppose, took over the language of *dikaios/dikaiosunē* from the Psalms when he developed his theology of 'justification (being made righteous) by faith (*pistis*)'. But *pistis* occurs hardly more than half a dozen times in all 150 Psalms. God's own faithfulness is normally indicated by *alētheia* (truthfulness), and human fidelity by *elpis* (hope). The Psalmist hopes in God, in the sense of trusting in God. In each case the words have the sense of faithfulness, of remaining loyal and sticking to it. The general idea is that of being righteous (i.e., having the status of being one of the righteous) through faithfulness. If Paul has taken his vocabulary from Psalms, why has he moved away from *elpis* to *pistis*? I suggest that it was to remain consistent with the two major Old Testament texts that he uses in Romans: at 1:17 from Habakkuk 2:4: 'the just man will live by faith' (or it might be translated 'the righteous man will live from faithfulness' – *Ho de dikaios ek pisteōs zēsetai*); and at Romans 4:9 from Genesis 15:6 about Abraham: 'faith was reckoned to Abraham as righteousness' (*Elogisthē tō Abraam hē pistis eis dikaio-sunēn*). In both these, his two principal citations in Romans, Paul uses forms of *pistis* for faith/faithfulness, rather than the Septuagint's *elpis*, hope. He departs from the Greek of the Psalms on this one point to maintain a consistency of vocabulary elsewhere in his citations.

What Paul is working towards in his use of Genesis is to show that Abraham, the founder of the Jewish people, was counted as a righteous man because he trusted God and believed God's promises: to have innumerable descendants and a land for them to live in, even though he was old and close to death, with a wife who was said to be ninety years old. This was confirmed and generalised by the prophet Habakkuk who said that the righteous man (and not just Abraham) will have life through his faith. Abraham's justification had nothing to do with keeping Torah because it happened long before Moses was given the law on Mount Sinai. What this means for Paul is that his fellow Christ-believing Jews and Gentiles can knowingly revert to an earlier time, before the giving of the law, by belonging to God's covenant by virtue of their faith (*pistis*) in God's promises, irrespective of what appeared later in the Torah. Christians can count Abraham as their father in faith and set Moses to one side. Paul came to think that the deficiency of synagogue-Judaism is that it holds to a temporary arrangement, the time of Torah, instead of reverting to a more distant past as a way of moving into the future. But we are not going to follow Paul's argument that far yet. We are still with the Psalms.

Righteousness in the Psalms is not only a question of status before God – being one of God's people, in the covenant – which is after all a technical matter. It also involves morality. To remain righteous one must do good things. God has to demonstrate his righteousness and so do his people. At this point you would expect the Psalmist to introduce the law as a measure of how we can do good actions. There are, however, surprisingly few uses of 'law' in the Psalms. Most references are to the negative *anomia*, lawlessness. In terms of a word-count, there is only limited evidence in the Psalms for righteousness/justification through fidelity to the law. What references there are include the promise that 'Happy [Blessed] are those who do not follow the advice of the wicked … but their delight is in the law of the Lord' (Psalm 1:2). While Psalm 88/89:30ff sounds a warning to those who break the law:

> If his [David's] children forsake my law
>   and do not walk according to my ordinances,
> if they violate my statutes
>   and do not keep my commandments;
> then I will punish their transgressions with the rod
>   and their iniquity with scourges;
> but I will not remove from him my steadfast love
>   or be false to my faithfulness.
> I will not violate my covenant
>   or alter the word that went forth from my lips.

However, if the language of law/*nomos* is not extensive, the long Psalm 118/119 more than compensates as a paean to God's law with its repeated admonitions to keep his commandments and ordinances, sayings (*logia*) and just judgements (*dikaiōmata*). Here there is certainly an overwhelming sense of being righteous/just by putting God's law into action.

Again we do not find much use of 'works' as such, but the Book of Psalms has a clear sense that God will reward and punish according to one's actions: 'you will repay to all according to their work' (61/62:12; see also 27/28:4–5). The Psalmist summarises his theology as follows:

The eyes of the Lord are on the righteous,
    and his ears are open to their cry.
The face of the Lord is against evildoers,
    to cut off the remembrance of them from the earth.
When the righteous cry for help, the Lord hears,
    and rescues them from all their troubles.
The Lord is near to the broken-hearted,
    and saves the crushed in spirit.
Many are the afflictions of the righteous
    but the Lord rescues them from them all.
He keeps all their bones;
    not one of them will be broken.
Evil brings death to the wicked,
    and those who hate the righteous will be condemned.
The Lord redeems the life of his servants;
    none of those who take refuge in him will be condemned.
(33/34:15–22)

Happy [Blessed] are those who ... do righteousness at all times. (105/106:3)

At the end of all this it is clear that Paul was able to find the concepts of 'law' and 'works' in the Book of Psalms, though in relation to righteousness he makes rather more of them than the Psalmist does. He also found there the language of 'sin', 'wrath', 'righteousness' and 'faithfulness' that he could use to similar, but in the end rather different, effect in Romans. There is certainly a doctrine of 'righteousness through faithfulness' in the Psalms and, as we have said, the markers of that faithfulness are the avoidance of idolatry and observance of the law. Circumcision, it might be added, is not an explicit issue there, though it became one for the emergent church by the middle of the first century AD. If we turn to the opening two chapters of Romans, we find Paul speculating on the fate of Gentiles and Jews in the light of their current behaviour. He paints a grim picture of both groups being destined for condemnation when they come to God's judgement – first the Jews and then the Gentiles, for God shows no partiality (Romans 2:10f). This is what Paul calls 'the wrath of God'. In doing this, he seems to be doing little more than adopting the Psalmist's own doctrine of righteousness through faithfulness in which faithfulness to the covenant is demonstrated by holding to the requirements of the Torah. The one difference that Paul makes explicit at this point in Romans is that, while the Gentiles might not have the Torah, they do have God's natural law written, so to speak, on their hearts, and he makes it clear that they should be able to see God, the creator, present in creation. So in behaving as Paul alleges they behave in chapter 1, the Gentiles are without any excuse. Paul has taken this theology from Wisdom 13—14. And Jews, who have the Torah, will be condemned for not keeping it (Romans 2). Having the law is not enough. Nor is it enough to be one of God's elect people. By the end of chapter 2, then, the final prospects for the human race do not look good. All are destined for the wrath of God because of their collective failure in faithfulness: to God, to his covenant and his Torah (for the Jews) and to natural moral law (for Gentiles).

5

Faithfulness II

The first two chapters of Romans do not fit easily with a Lutheran understanding of justification by faith. The basic idea of Luther in his reading of Paul is that while everyone without exception deserves God's wrath because of their subjection to and co-operation with sin, God will justify those who have faith in Christ. This means that God will not hold our failure to perform good actions ('works') against us if we believe that God in his supreme generosity has done everything necessary in Christ to reconcile us to himself. In Paul Tillich's words, this is 'the acceptance of acceptance'. We have to accept that God accepts us as we are with all our failings. This is a wonderful message (if it is true) and exactly characterises the God of Christianity. It indicates that in Christ God speaks to those who are failures in the world and says that it doesn't matter. Salvation comes through trusting God and not through performing morally successful actions, i.e., good works. Indeed Luther went so far as to affirm that no matter how vigorously we do perform good works, these are human achievements that will never compensate for our debt to sin and win us favour with God. What we need is faith, not works.

This can be a liberating idea: that our moral failures do not cut us off from God irrevocably. But it is not easy to reconcile this understanding with what Paul writes in Romans 1:18—3:20 where Gentiles and Jews are indeed said to be judged on their behaviour: Gentiles will be judged on whether they have kept the natural moral law, which can be discovered through creation (1:19–21 with a list of their faults in the following verses); and Jews on whether they have kept the law that God has given them (2:1, 12–13). So how can we reconcile Luther's understanding of justification outlined in the paragraph above with the following passage?

> For he will repay according to each one's deeds: to those who by patiently doing good seek for glory and honour and immortality, he will give eternal life; while for those who are self-seeking and who obey not the truth but wickedness, there will be wrath and fury. There will be anguish and distress for everyone who does evil, the Jew first and also the Greek, but glory and honour and peace for everyone who does good, the Jew first and also the Greek. For God shows no partiality. All who have sinned apart from the law will also perish apart from the law, and all who have sinned under the law will be judged by the law. For it is not the hearers of the law who are righteous in God's sight, but the doers of the law who will be justified [made righteous]. When gentiles, who do not possess the law, do instinctively what the law requires, these, though not having the law, are a law to themselves. They show that what the law requires is written on their hearts, to which their own conscience also bears witness. (2:6–15).

Clearly the two do not fit: in Luther, belief alone leads to being counted righteous, while in the quotation above from Paul, all are to be judged by their actions. To get out of this we could suppose that Paul is not a coherent thinker, which is a view we should regard as a last resort only if all else fails. E. P. Sanders comes close to holding this view. He can find no inner unity that holds together Paul's various statements about the law. On the passage quoted above he says,

> Even at the point at which Paul may most obviously be charged with true incoherence, the statements in Romans 2 that the sole basis of salvation is fulfilment of the law, we can see that he has been led to make use of material which is contrary to one of his central convictions (salvation by faith in Jesus Christ) by the desire to assert another one (the equality of Jew and Gentile). Nevertheless Romans 2 remains the

instance in which Paul goes beyond inconsistency or variety of argument and explanation to true self-contradiction.[1]

Or we might suppose, like Douglas Campbell, that Paul is here giving an account of his *opponent's* position, that of a fictive non-Christian Jewish teacher, whose argument Paul is about to dismantle in what follows.[2] Yet chapters 1—2 do not read as though Paul is expounding someone else's position. So it would be more satisfactory if we were able to work out a third position in which chapters 1—2 express Paul's own stance but understood in a way that preserves the inner coherence of the letter, especially between chapters 1—2 and 3—4.

Righteousness in Romans 1:1—3:20

The German Evangelical tradition, which has produced so many great theologians, has always emphasised Martin Luther's distinction between Judaism and Christianity, which Luther himself characterised as a distinction between 'law' and 'gospel'. What we find in this first section of Romans, however (after the introduction, 1:1–17), seems to be thoroughly Jewish, expressing a doctrine of salvation based on rewards and punishments for behaviour. The one advantage Jews have over Gentiles is that God has given them the Law/Torah for their moral education. In effect we find here the doctrine of righteousness that Paul would have found in the Psalms, which we outlined in the previous chapter. Far from rejecting his Jewish inheritance, Paul has used it as a framework for developing a new understanding of 'righteousness through faithfulness' (*dikaiosunē dia pistin*), as I shall now rather inelegantly call what has usually been known as justification by faith. He uses the ideas and the Greek vocabulary that he found in the Psalms of the Septuagint, with the one exception of the language of faith or faithfulness replacing that

---

1   E. P. Sanders, *Paul, the Law, and the Jewish People* (London: SCM Press, 1985), p.147.

2   Douglas Campbell, *The Quest for Paul's Gospel* (London: T&T Clark International, 2005), ch. 11, 'Reading Romans 1:8 – 3:20', pp. 233–61. This view can also be found in Part Four of his more recent *The Deliverance of God* (Grand Rapids, MI: Eerdmans, 2009).

of hope (*elpis* to *pistis*). So, to understand Paul, it is important to refer to the text of the Greek Bible that he was using, and also to read the Psalms as a block, as Paul would have done, without much sense of their original historical contexts and development. In order to preserve what I take to be the influence of the Psalms on Paul, I shall normally translate *dikaiosunē* as 'righteousness' and *pistis* as 'faithfulness' with fidelity, trust and perhaps loyalty as acceptable alternatives. Occasionally *pistis* has to be translated 'faith' though only, I suggest, when the content of belief is being indicated, such as believing in or having faith in the resurrection, for example.

Let us see how all this makes a difference to Paul's introduction (1:1–15). He begins with a personal introduction to those in Rome, to whom he says that he is 'set apart for the gospel of God ... concerning his Son ... Jesus Christ our Lord, through whom we have received grace and apostleship to bring about the obedience of faith among all the Gentiles ... including yourselves'. He thanks God for them 'because your faithfulness is proclaimed throughout the world' (1:8) and Paul adds that he longs to see them in Rome 'so that we may be mutually encouraged by each other's faithfulness' (1:12). He then begins his argument proper with a programmatic statement at 1:16–17 in which again I modify the translation of the NRSV to show how 'faithfulness' works at least as well as and actually better than 'faith'.

> For I am not ashamed of the gospel; it is the power of God for salvation for everyone who shows faithfulness, to the Jew first and also to the Greek. For in it the righteousness of God is revealed through faithfulness for faithfulness; as it is written [in Habakkuk 2:4], 'The one who is righteous will live by faithfulness.'

I do not think Paul intended those two sentences to be immediately intelligible. They form a rhetorical statement in which he introduces many of the key words that will become important later in the letter.

There is also an element of rhetoric in the section that follows, in which Paul lists the many and varied sins that we find among Gentiles and Jews, all deserving God's wrath, we are told. This is very much the view of righteousness that we find in the long Psalm 118/119. Could we, then, be reading an account of the Jewish way of righteousness that Paul actually rejects, as Campbell suggests? This is unlikely for two reasons. First, Paul introduces the theme of the equality of Jew and Gentile in 2:9b–11 and, second, because Jesus Christ is brought in at 2:16, neither of which would come from a synagogue-Jew. I suggest that chapter 2 is best read as Paul himself addressing a fictive Jewish reader (that is, a non-Christian Jew rather than one of the so-called Judaising Christians) and warning him of what is to come from not living up to the expectations of the Psalms and the Torah generally, namely that Jews must demonstrate their righteousness through faithfulness to God's covenant by keeping the law.

Faithfulness is how both the RSV and NRSV translate the opening of chapter 3: 'What if some [Jews] were unfaithful? Will their faithlessness nullify the faithfulness of God?' (3.3). Of course, there is nothing anti-Jewish in alleging that some Jews have been unfaithful to the covenant. It is a theme that runs through the prophets. Does their unfaithfulness cancel out God's faithfulness? No, but in what way might their (and our) unrighteousness confirm the righteousness of God, which is what Paul pushes towards in 3:5? Only if there is an unstated assumption that God proves his righteousness by inflicting his wrath on all who have been unrighteous. Again this is the view of the Psalms: God is righteous and remains faithful to his covenant; he rewards righteous Jews who show the same faithfulness and he punishes the unrighteous/unfaithful, whether they are Jews or not. The Psalms assume that by definition Gentiles cannot be righteous because they are not members of God's covenant people and they do not worship the God of Abraham, Isaac and Joseph, i.e., they are idolatrous. At this point in Romans 3 Paul produces a cluster of quotations from the Psalms (and one line from Isaiah) to show that in reality no one is righteous before God and that *everyone* deserves God's wrath.[3] This last conclusion does not seem at all Jewish but Paul is certain that his position is scriptural. However, this is not the end of Paul's argument.

---

3 Psalms 14:1–2; 53:1–2; 5:9; 140:3; 10:7; 36:1; and Isa. 59:7–8.

Paul's Shift in the Doctrine of Righteousness at Romans 3:21

At this point Paul makes his move away from the theology of the Psalms by shifting, with a flexibility and seeming arbitrariness that the modern reader might well find surprising, from 'No one will be counted righteous before him' (Psalm 142/143:2) to 'No one will be counted righteous before him *by works of the law*' (Romans 3:20) where the italicised words have been added by Paul. This is because Paul believes that 'the righteousness of God has now been revealed apart from the law ... the righteousness of God through the faithfulness of Jesus Christ for all who are themselves faithful' (3:21f). Paul has kept the framework of the doctrine of righteousness that he found in the Psalms but from this verse onwards everything is *christologised*. Faithfulness to Christ has replaced faithfulness to the law as the mark of one's righteousness. This is his one major change to what he found in the Psalms but it is the change that changes everything.

One can only speculate about what it was that triggered this shift but it is possible that it was Paul's meditating on Psalm 36/37:39, 'The salvation of the righteous is from the Lord', where, for Paul and the early church, the Lord is now Jesus Christ. And perhaps also from a Christian understanding of 'The Lord is righteous' (Psalm 10:8/11:7; 144/145:17), for while *Kurios* (Lord) was used in the Greek Bible for God's special name given to Moses from the burning bush (Exodus 3:14), in the New Testament it is the title given to Jesus Christ. It is a use which reflects Christian belief in the incarnation. As we shall see in the final chapter, Paul dealt with the distinction between Father and Son in the godhead by addressing the Father and Creator as *theos* (God) and the Son as *kurios* (Lord). At any rate the righteousness and faithfulness attributed to God in the Jewish Bible (Old Testament) are now attributed to Jesus in the New Testament.

Paul shows us in Romans that his model of faithfulness is the righteous one, the Lord, Jesus Christ. Jesus proved his righteousness by remaining faithful to his God-given task right to the end and was raised from the dead by his Father as a reward for him and a proof for us. The resurrection is the ultimate vindication of God's righteousness. This is why for Paul the resurrection is at the centre of that to which we must hold fast: righteousness 'will be reckoned to us who believe in him who raised Jesus our Lord from the dead, who was handed over to death for our trespasses and raised so we could be counted righteous' (Romans 4:24f). Before the coming of Christ, Jews showed their righteousness by remaining faithful to God and keeping his law; now all people – Jews and Gentiles, men and women, slaves and free (Galatians 3:27f) – show their righteousness by holding fast to the God who raised Jesus from the dead. In a difficult line, Paul says that we should no longer attempt to ascend to heaven to find the Lord, nor descend into Hades, for he is here in front of us in Jesus Christ, the risen one (Romans 10:6–9, in which Paul gives a Christian interpretation to Deuteronomy 30:12–14).

This comes in a lengthy section where Paul agonises over the fate of his own people, for whose sake, he says, he would even be 'accursed and cut off from Christ' (9:3) – a statement we find difficult to take literally. His people continue to hold a privileged position:

> They are Israelites, and to them belong the adoption [by God], the glory, the covenants, the giving of the law, the worship, and the promises, to them belong the patriarchs, and from them, according to the flesh, comes the Messiah. (9:4f)

But now they are no longer counted righteous. They still have the law and it remains God's gift. Yet Paul is not criticising the Jews at this point for flouting the law as he did in chapter 2. Being righteous is a question of one's status before God and they have lost it. Their problem is that

> Gentiles, who did not strive for righteousness, have attained it, that is, righteousness through faith/trust; but Israel, who did strive for the righteousness that is based on the law, did not succeed in fulfilling that law. Why not? Because they did not strive for it on the basis of faith/trust, but as if it were based on works. (9:30–32)

(This is one place where *pistis* is not best translated as 'faithfulness', for here it seems to have the sense of 'trust' as when Abraham in

Genesis trusted God's promises.) Holding to the law might once have been the way of showing one's faithfulness to God but things have now shifted in God's grand scheme of things. The faithfulness that now counts, according to Paul, is faithfulness to Christ. One might ask whether God has been unfair in changing his scheme for salvation by sending his son and inadvertently catching out the Jews, but Paul's point is that attaining righteousness through faithfulness to the law was not working anyway. In striving for 'the righteousness that is based on the law', the problem for the Jews is that they are 'striving' rather than being receptive to God's mercy, unlike the Gentiles (those Gentiles who have become Christ-believers), and they are striving for something they can never succeed in fulfilling completely because of the destructive power of sin, as Paul tries to show in 7:7–24. They are aiming for righteousness using the wrong measure of faithfulness.

Even in Galatians where Paul is very negative about the law, it may be that he does not think that the law is finished with. The key passage is Galatians 2:16 which appears to contrast law and faith, and which gives the idea that faith involves believing things about Jesus. It hints at, if not a narrowly intellectual understanding of faith, at least an idea of faith as something that goes on in your head. It may not exactly involve believing six impossible things before breakfast as the White Queen claimed she could to Alice, but it seems to involve believing things about Jesus which might not be obvious to others. NRSV translates it as follows:

> we know that a person is justified not by works of the law but through faith in Jesus Christ (*ean mē dia pisteōs Iēsou Christou*). And we have come to believe in Christ Jesus, so that we might be justified by faith in Christ, and not by doing the works of the law, because no one will be justified by the works of the law.

Pursuing the line taken in this chapter so far, I suggest that we will understand these two sentences better if we render 'justified' as 'counted righteous'. 'Faith' should become 'faithfulness'. *Ean mē* , translated here as 'but' to emphasise the contrast between law and faith, should be given its normal meaning of 'unless'. And then – a matter of some controversy but following the trend of recent Pauline criticism – *pisteōs Iēsou Christou* should not be translated as an objective genitive, 'faith in Jesus Christ', but as a subjective genitive, 'the faith of Jesus Christ' or, better, 'the faithfulness of Jesus Christ'. The whole passage then becomes:

> We are Jews ... knowing that a person is not *counted righteous* from works of the law *unless* through the *faithfulness of* Jesus Christ, and we have remained *faithful* to Christ Jesus so that we might be *counted righteous* from the *faithfulness of* Christ and not from works of the law, because [as scripture says] 'no one will be *counted righteous*' from works of the law.

We are no longer counted righteous through faith in the head, as it were, but through faithfulness in life. This translation also reduces the opposition between the law and faith and allows a glimmer of the more positive attitude to the law that Paul expresses in Romans. It suggests that keeping the law as such is not the problem, but keeping it as though it could lead to righteousness *apart from Christ*. There is actually a sense in which keeping the law does show our righteousness, provided it follows on from faithfulness to Jesus Christ. Here Jesus is the model of what faithfulness should be, a faithfulness that we are invited to copy. Jesus' faithfulness was to his God-given mission; our faithfulness is to him in the way we live out our lives. We cannot prove that this is what Paul intended in Galatians 2:16 but this reading does move towards a more consistent and coherent understanding of Paul across both Galatians and Romans. And it is an understanding that gets round an unfortunate dualism between what we might call faith in the head and faithfulness in life.

So what is the place of the law in Paul's scheme? There has been a huge debate about this which still goes on. It is not a narrowly academic debate; it is about the place of law in the Christian life and how it might determine one's behaviour. Resolution of the debate has been made difficult by Paul's own different emphases (not inconsistency) in the different social contexts that lie behind Galatians and Romans. Put simply, Paul is very negative about the Jewish law in Galatians where he had to argue against Judaising Christians.

These were Christian Pharisees who were based in Jerusalem, allegedly under the leadership of James 'the Lord's brother', who believed that all Christians should abide by the law of Moses, including the practice of circumcision as commanded in Genesis 17. And this despite the decision of the Apostolic Council held in Jerusalem in AD 48, as reported in Acts 15 and Galatians 2. In Romans, however, where this problem was not in evidence, Paul takes a much more positive view of the Jewish law. He calls it a gift from God (9:4), containing 'just requirements' (8:4). It is spiritual (7:14) and it is certainly not to be identified with sin (7:7), even though its prohibitions might provoke us into sinning because of our own captivity to the power of sin (7:7ff). On the one hand, the church decided at a very early stage not to abide by all the requirements of the Torah (Acts 15). On the other hand Paul's positive comments on the law in Romans show that the law is not a bad thing in itself but a weak thing, incapable of fulfilment (even though Paul claimed that in his former life he was blameless under the law, Philippians 3:6) and not the vehicle of salvation and reconciliation with God. Paul was no antinomian, i.e., he was not a complete libertarian. Nor was Luther, but his creation of a theological antithesis between law and gospel (representing Judaism and Christianity) was unfortunate and his antagonism to the law was wide of the mark.

Between those two theological extremes – Christian acceptance of the law in its entirety (Judaisers) and rejection of it in its entirety (antinomians and, in a rather different way, Luther) – lies the recent suggestion from Tom Wright and James Dunn that it is the ritual 'boundary markers' of Judaism that have been abrogated, while the Torah's moral law still stands.[4] So circumcision, the food laws and

---

4 J. D. G. Dunn, *Jesus, Paul and the Law* (London: SPCK, 1990), pp. 191–5; and *The Theology of Paul the Apostle* (Edinburgh: T&T Clark, 1998), pp. 354–66; N. T. Wright, 'New Perspectives on Paul', a paper from the 10th Edinburgh Dogmatics Conference, August 2003, section 4 'Ordo Salutis' on www.nt-wrightpage.com. Dunn and Wright might be surprised to discover that they are supported by St Thomas Aquinas, though he was not discussing Paul specifically: 'Lex nova non evacuat observantiam veteris legis nisi quantum ad caeremonialia' (the new law does not exclude observation of the old law except

purification rites are out, while the prohibitions on murder, adultery and the rest still apply. Boundary markers are those public rites that indicate who is within the community and who is outside. They are essentially tribal. In a universal religion like Christianity open to all races, social classes and sexes, they are inappropriate and divisive. There are as a historical fact no such observable identity markers for those who are in the church. The criteria for being in are belief (ritualised in baptism) and a serious attempt to live the Christian life. The problem with boundary markers is that they separate and exclude, and division within the church was something Paul struggled against all his life as a Christian.

Can we draw a legitimate distinction between ritual instructions and moral laws as Wright and Dunn suggest? Paul himself makes no explicit distinction between two forms of law so that part of the Torah becomes redundant but not the rest. Nor does he suggest that Jewish Christians like himself might continue to keep all the legal requirements of the Torah, while Gentile Christians can be excused the ritual demands on cultural grounds. Paul thinks we have *all* been released from the demands of the law (Romans 7:6) and the implication seems to be that Christian believers have been released from *all* the demands of the law. At the same time, Paul does not think we can then do anything we like – it is still wrong to murder, steal and so on, and the particular example he uses in Romans 7 is that of coveting. In a not especially convincing argument at the beginning of Romans 7, Paul says that the law which binds a husband or wife to their spouse is effective only during their lifetime. If one dies, the survivor is discharged from the law that bound them. He then compares this to the situation of Jews and the law. He says that a death has taken place – Christ on the cross – and Jews are no longer bound by the law. The analogy does not work exactly, but Paul's point is that the time of the law is up. We have moved into a period where the law is no longer relevant. It was valid for a time (from Moses to Christ); it has not now been abolished; it

---

insofar as it concerns rituals), *Summa Theologiae* 2a, 107.2 ad 1. However, he does go on to say that the words of Christ are all that is needed for salvation (108.2 sed contra).

has not become objectionable; nor is it the case that some of it stands and the rest is disposable. *All* of it now falls into the background and becomes beside the point in this new age. It is redundant, it has been superseded.

It is not just the law that we have moved beyond. We have been freed from the law–sin–death axis that has oppressed humanity and it has been replaced by a regime of grace–holiness–life. As he says, 'The life I now live in the flesh I live by faithfulness to the son of God who loved me and gave himself for me' (Galatians 2:20). In Philippians he says that he is confident of his blamelessness 'according to the righteousness which is in the law', yet he adds that it will no longer do to have 'my own righteousness which is from the law, but one which is through the faithfulness of Christ, the righteousness of God which is founded upon faithfulness' (Philippians 3:6, 9).

There remains the problem of how to translate Romans 10:4 where Christ is said to be the *telos* or end of the law, where *telos* can mean either termination or goal. So has Christ ended/terminated the law, or has he brought it to its fulfilment/goal? The fact is that both are right. The time of the law as a mark of faithfulness has come to an end, and the law has all the time been leading towards Christ as its goal. I think this is clear when we read the whole line: 'For Christ is the end (*telos*) of the law so that there may be righteousness for everyone who believes', i.e., Jews *and* Gentiles.

How Do We Now Become Righteous?

Justification by faith is usually thought to be the quintessence of Pauline theology. Yet Paul did not invent the doctrine of what I now call righteousness through faithfulness. He found it in the Book of Psalms – though it is typical of the Old Testament as a whole – and reworked its framework and most of its vocabulary, first in Galatians and then in a more developed way in Romans, finally transforming it utterly by christologising it. It is this christologisation that is essentially Pauline. The value of the law in itself remains, though its effectiveness to make one holy had always been corrupted by sin (present from the beginning of the human race and represented by Adam), and trying to keep the law now apart from faithfulness to Jesus Christ is futile. According to Paul, the law never did get you very far, and now that something immeasurably better is available, it gets you nowhere. Paul thought that it never did get Jews as far as they hoped it would; it did more to educate them in the ways of sin than keep them from it (rather like the effect of sending someone to prison). It is the law-apart-from-Christ that Paul criticises. However, in Galatians and Romans being righteous is not the same as being saved, so where does righteousness fit into the broader scheme of salvation?

For Paul, being righteous is still a matter of status before God rather than having achieved moral excellence, though *remaining* righteous involves not falling back into sin.

> Should we continue in sin in order that grace may abound? By no means! How can we who died to sin go on living in it? Do you not know that all of us who have been baptized into Christ Jesus were baptized into his death? Therefore we have been buried with him by baptism into death, so that, just as Christ was raised from the dead by the glory of the Father, so we too might walk in newness of life. (Romans 6:1–4)

In the context of asking who one might die for, Paul distinguishes three levels of being-human, in ascending order: the sinner, the righteous person and the good person.

> Indeed rarely will anyone die for a righteous person – though perhaps for a good person someone might actually dare to die. But God proves his love for us in that while we were still sinners Christ died for us. (5:7–8)

Being righteous, then, is not the end of the line; it is one step on from being a sinner but it is not as advanced as being good. If we track through the verses that follow we find that when sin has been left behind (i.e., idolatry and law breaking) we become righteous. This is a state confirmed by baptism. It is not the most exalted state but in context seems to be equivalent to 'reconciliation', a state we can experience at the present time.

> Much more surely then, now that we have been justified/ made righteous by his blood [i.e., by his death], will we be

saved through him from the wrath of God. For if while we were enemies, we were reconciled to God through the death of his Son, much more surely, having been reconciled, will we be saved by his life. But more than that, we even boast in God through our Lord Jesus Christ, through whom we have now received reconciliation. (5:9–11)

So having been made righteous and reconciled with God, having found newness of life, we are given a promise for the future that 'we will be saved from the wrath of God'. For this to be brought to fruition we must remain faithful to the end, a state Paul characterises as obedience, what he calls 'the obedience of faith' – though by this stage you might prefer to call it the obedience of faithfulness (1:5; 16:26). Through remaining faithful we move towards becoming a good person, towards holiness. We become, in Paul's sense, a saint (1:7; 16:2). This is the process of sanctification and it may well involve suffering.

For just as you once presented your members as slaves to impurity and to greater and greater iniquity, so now present your members as slaves to righteousness for sanctification. (6:19)

… we suffer with him so that we may also be glorified with him. I consider that the sufferings of this present time are not worth comparing with the glory about to be revealed to us. (8:17–18)

If we remain faithful to the end, it will lead to eternal life (5:21; 6:23) and resurrection from the dead (6:5).

All this amplifies the fourth and fifth stages of Paul's fivefold scheme found in Romans 8:29–30: foreknown – predestined – called – made righteous – glorified.

For those whom he foreknew he also predestined to be conformed to the image of his Son, in order that he might be the firstborn within a large family. And those whom he predestined he also called; and those whom he called he also justified/made righteous; and those whom he justified/made righteous he also glorified.

The law might be good in itself but there is no place for it here as it is not something of any great relevance for the new humanity of Jews and Gentiles who are together 'in Christ'. Augustine was right to say that we should love and do as we wish because if we remain faithful to Christ and truly love as he did, then we shall find ourselves fulfilling the law, or as much of it as is still relevant in this new age.

Does this mean that belief in Christ has superseded Judaism, which is a very unpopular thing to suggest these days, something that is not at all politically correct? In one sense the answer is 'no' because from Paul's perspective this debate was and is taking place within Jewish religious tradition. In Paul's time there only was Judaism and paganism (itself a complex of religious traditions). But in another sense Paul certainly thinks that belief in Christ has superseded the Torah because it is now through faithfulness to Christ that we become righteous and are destined for sanctification and salvation.

The new scheme of things is as follows:

> God shows his righteousness by being faithful to the promises he had made, and these were fulfilled in the coming of Jesus Christ;

> Jesus shows his righteousness by being faithful to his mission, by seeing it through to the end, 'obedient to the point of death, even death on a cross' (and exaltation, Philippians 2:8–11) – in this he offers us a model to be copied;

> We become righteous through faithfulness to Christ and remaining faithful to the end, even if it involves suffering and death (and resurrection, 1 Corinthians 15).

At this point other things come together. It may be that Paul developed the idea of slavery in Romans, a theme we explored in an earlier chapter, because the slave is an exemplar of faithfulness and obedience. These are qualities that Paul recommends in his other letters too, most clearly in Colossians 1:21–23:

> You who were once estranged and hostile in mind, doing evil deeds, he [Christ] has now reconciled in his fleshly body through death, so as to present you holy and blameless and irreproachable before him – provided that you continue securely established and steadfast in the faith, without shifting from the hope promised by the gospel that you heard, which has been proclaimed to every creature under heaven.

Fidelity

It has become clear from this complex theology that faithfulness is at the centre of those moral qualities that characterise the Christian life. It may at times seem that the discussion of righteousness and justification is part of an archaic and even arcane academic debate. After all, it is not the language of everyday conversation. The oddness and perhaps old-fashioned quality of the language has to stay, however, for there seems no other way of rendering Paul's Greek, though it might help readers if we were sometimes to render 'faithfulness' by an equivalent such as trust or loyalty or, depending on context, fidelity. Fidelity is not a narrowly religious attribute. It spills into many aspects of life. It concerns husbands and wives, parents and children, friendships, voluntary societies, colleagues at work, and even loyalty to one's nation. Yet it is a disposition that we have great difficulty with in modern Western society. It is not only a younger generation that finds it uncongenial to make commitments and stick to them, but for them it seems to be particularly difficult. This reluctance to commit shows itself not only in weak religious allegiances but in relationships generally, especially between young men and women. Society is the worse for this but, in appealing for a rediscovery of the importance of fidelity, we need to utter a word of caution. For Paul, fidelity is related to obedience and what he understands by slavery. People have good reason to have reservations about any call to obedient submission. Obeying orders can lead to war crimes; obeying one's employer can lead to financial crimes and social injustice; obeying one's husband can bring humiliation, servility and maybe injury. We seem to be between the devil and the deep blue sea: commitment, fidelity and obedience, or withholding commitment and failing to remain faithful. Yet it does not have to be all or nothing. Commitments have to be entered into with foresight. Our commitments have to be tested by rational argument so that we make the right commitments, commitments that lead to our flourishing as human beings. Then perhaps we will succeed in seeing our commitments through to the end. We might call this the intellectualism of faith. For fidelity is without doubt an essential component in Paul's account of the Christian life.

6

Hope

The Christian Life as a Life of Suffering

You would expect that a life modelled on faithfulness to Christ would bring pain as well as joy. As the pessimistic author of 2 Timothy says, 'all who want to live a godly life in Christ Jesus will be persecuted' (3:12). The theme of suffering runs through Paul's letters and it is a theme that connects Paul to Christ (and before him to Jeremiah and Isaiah, especially chapter 53) and to his own fellow believers. Life, of course, brings suffering but the Christian gospel is not to be chosen as a form of escapism. Paul thinks that in some ways it accentuates suffering.

Some of Paul's own pain was contingent on the circumstances of his life and rooted in how he was received in a few of his own communities, particularly Galatia and Corinth. The problem in Galatia was the influence of the so-called Judaisers who thought Christian believers were obliged to keep all the requirements of the Mosaic law: circumcision, Sabbath, food laws, purity rituals, sacrifice and all the rest. Relations became acrimonious and it has to be said that in his language to them Paul gave as good as he got, showing exasperation in places (Galatians 5:7–12). His problem with the Christians in Corinth was that when he met them he failed to meet their expectations of what a religious or philosophical teacher should be like: eloquent, a man of stature, full of charm and wit. Apollos seems to have met their standards better. Initially Paul was well received but their goodwill soon dissipated (1 Corinthians 4:12f).

While some of Paul's pain was caused by his own fellow Christians, his deepest suffering came from his activities as an apostle and missionary in response to the call to take the gospel to the furthest corner of the Roman Empire. In Romans 9—11 Paul suggests that the time for him to complete this task was very short. He must rush to take the 'good news' to all the Gentiles, for only then would God turn again to the Jews, who have been cut off for a time because of their 'disobedience'. He likens this to branches cut from a tree that can be grafted back in their original position on to the trunk. That gospel was the message of a small Jewish sect who made improbable claims about their leader – that he had been crucified and raised from the dead – a message which had decidedly anti-imperial overtones: their one Lord and Saviour is Jesus Christ, not the emperor, and their citizenship is in heaven rather than this world. The state found their ritual practice suspect because they would not follow the religious conventions of civil obedience by sacrificing to the emperor. It is in this general context that Paul lists what he has had to undergo in his life as an apostle: arrests and imprisonments, innumerable floggings which often brought him near to death; he tells us he had five times received the thirty-nine lashes from the Jews (this was so punishing that it was thought forty might be fatal); three times he was beaten with rods, once there was a stoning, and he had been shipwrecked three times which on one occasion left him adrift at sea for a full day and night. Then he lists his general labours: there had been frequent journeys with danger from swollen rivers, from bandits, from his own people and from Gentiles, he had been in danger from the sea and deserts, from false brothers, 'in toil and hardship, through many a sleepless night … often without food, cold and naked … under daily pressure because of my anxiety for all the churches' (2 Corinthians 11:23–28; see also 6:4f). Such was the life of an apostle. At any rate such was Paul's life by the time he wrote this letter around AD 55. Small wonder, then, that his letters contain numerous references to suffering, persecution, distress and mistreatments, even his earliest letter (1 Thessalonians 2:2; 3:7).

Paul went through all this to take the gospel round the Mediterranean to the north and west of Jerusalem. In the mid-50s he introduced himself by letter to the church in Rome, a community he had neither founded nor visited, announcing that he hoped to see them on his way to Spain, his ultimate destination. He got to Rome eventually – under arrest – though never to Spain. Imprisonment was not a new experience for him. There seem to have been a number of these, though there is a good deal of doubt about the historical details. Acts mentions three: the first was in Philippi (Acts 16) and the second in Caesarea (Acts 24—25) before he was sent on to Rome where he perished in the time of Nero (Acts 27—28). In the words that Luke has put into Paul's mouth, 'the Holy Spirit testifies to me in every city that imprisonment and persecutions are waiting for me.' Yet he counts his life as nothing so long as he can fulfil his vocation as an apostle 'to testify to the good news of God's grace' (Acts 20:23f). Indeed in Philippians he seems almost to welcome his imprisonment as it has made it known to the imperial guard (is in this Rome?) that he was being detained for speaking boldly and fearlessly about Christ. In social terms the outcome was one of ignominy and rejection, both for him and for other believers in a similar position. Earlier he had told the Corinthians that they have become 'a spectacle to the world' as though they were sentenced to death. They are fools for Christ's sake, weak and held in disrepute. 'We have become like the rubbish of the world, the dregs of all things' (1 Corinthians 4:9–13). And still he asks those in Corinth to be his imitators!

Why did Paul go through all of this? It was entirely for the sake of his brothers and sisters in his churches (2 Corinthians 1:5–7), both in order to bring them the gospel while he still had time (Philippians 1:18), and to identify with Christ in his suffering (Colossians 1:24). 'For his sake I have suffered the loss of all things, and I regard them as rubbish [literally: crap], in order that I may gain Christ and be found in him' (Philippians 3:8f).

The gospel was Paul's pearl of great price for which everything else has to be given up. Surprisingly, Paul does not refer directly to the sufferings of Christ very often, though he has frequent allusions to the cross. Romans 5:8 tells us that Christ died for us while we were still sinners, which proves God's love for us, and Paul occasionally speaks of the benefits derived from the 'blood' of the cross without dwelling on the details of that torturous and ignominious execution. Although Paul puts Christ-crucified at the centre of his message, he prefers to speak of the crucifixion dispassionately, almost as a symbol, though any first-century reader would have known the full horror of what was involved. Paul uses the symbol of the cross to show how the power of God resides in what the world regards as weakness and stupidity. Worshipping a crucified criminal is foolishness to a Greek who respects rationality and philosophy; worshipping a crucified messiah is an impossibility for a Jew, whose messiah would sit on the throne in a restored Jerusalem. But 'Christ crucified' is God's repudiation of conventional social and religious expectations:

> to those who are the called, both Jews and Greeks, Christ [is] the power of God and the wisdom of God. For God's foolishness is wiser than human wisdom, and God's weakness is stronger than human strength. (1 Corinthians 1:24f)

Paul did not regard himself as a living martyr, suffering heroically for his fellow believers (though Colossians 1:24 has the curious reference to his 'completing what is lacking in Christ's afflictions for the sake of his body, that is, the church' – which would hardly count as orthodox doctrine in a later century). He thought they too would take an active part in this kind of life by virtue of their having been baptised into Christ, and so into a share in his suffering. The first letter to the Thessalonians refers to their persecutions and speaks of them having become imitators of Paul and 'the Lord', though at the same time imitation brings joy from the Holy Spirit (1 Thessalonians 1:6; 2:14). Romans too presupposes a life of suffering, though in the end nothing can separate Paul and his fellow believers from Christ, whose glory will be incomparable (Romans 8:18, 35–39). In the meantime, they must be patient in their suffering (12:12).

The second letter to the Corinthians deserves a word to itself. Suffering is a theme that surfaces repeatedly in this letter, mainly because of the difficult relations Paul had with this community. As we have seen, he wrote four letters that we know of to Corinth, while he in turn received letters from and reports about them. First Corinthians is largely concerned with particular problems in Corinth that had been brought to his attention and general themes like suffering do not lie on the surface. This was followed by a letter that no longer survives, but caused the author great distress (2 Corinthians 2:4 refers to it) and shows that his relationship with them had gone downhill fast. By the closing chapters of 2 Corinthians there are clear indications that he had become really upset by their calumnies, their accusations of his boasting on his own behalf and their rejection of him as an apostle. Our interest, however, is not with these contingent problems but with the way Paul characterises the Christian life as a life that inexorably brings social rejection and possibly even persecution from society outside the church.

In places, when outlining his sufferings, Paul distinguishes what he is going through from the benefits that accrue to his brethren in Corinth: the sufferings of Christ are abundant in him for their consolation (1:3–7). The result, indeed the purpose, of this life of suffering is to show that one does not rely on one's own resources but on the strengthening power of God who brings consolation: 'we felt that we had received the sentence of death [in Asia] so that we would not rely on ourselves but on God who raises the dead' (1:9). He refers in 12:7 to the thorn that God has placed in his side, the precise nature of which still puzzles us, but which caused him so much pain that it stopped him thinking too well of himself and his 'achievements'. This 'thorn' alone would stop him boasting. However, the figure he cut seems to have been the actual reason the Corinthians rejected him, so unlike the conventional Hellenic view of what a teacher of religion or philosophy should be like. It has been suggested that they might have welcomed Paul initially because they thought there would be some social advantage to be gained from being associated with a teacher of stature. But when they met Paul in the flesh, they were disappointed. Apparently he lacked eloquence (which is surprising when you consider the quality of his writing) and may have looked physically damaged and exhausted. Yet he tried to turn this to his advantage by claiming that it was in suffering and weakness that he identified with Christ:

But we have this treasure in clay jars [i.e. our bodies], so that it may be made clear that this extraordinary power belongs to God and does not come from us. We are afflicted in every way, but not crushed; perplexed but not driven to despair; persecuted, but not forsaken; struck down, but not destroyed; always carrying in the body the death of Jesus, so that the life of Jesus may be made visible in our bodies. For while we live, we are always being given up to death for Jesus' sake, so that the life of Jesus may be made visible in our mortal flesh. (4:7–11)

So in rejecting Paul, the Corinthians were at the same time rejecting the pattern of Christ's life and showing a fundamental misunderstanding of what the Christian life is about.

A recent study by Kar Yong Lim has noted the particular influence of scripture in 2 Corinthians, especially Isaiah 49, which Paul quotes at 6:2 (as well as at Romans 14:11).[1] Isaiah 49 begins with the second of the 'suffering servant songs' and you can see immediately why Paul would identify with the servant and seek consolation in Isaiah's poem.

The Lord called me before I was born ... he made my mouth like a sharp sword ... he said to me, 'You are my servant, in whom I will be glorified.' But I said, 'I have laboured in vain, I have spent my strength for nothing and vanity; yet surely my cause is with the Lord, and my reward with my God.' (Isaiah 49:1–4)

God then responds,

It is too light a thing that you should be my servant
    to raise up the tribes of Jacob
    and to restore the survivors of Israel;
I will give you as a light to the nations,
    that my salvation may reach to the end of the earth. (49:6)

Paul would have seen this as a word addressed to him and we can detect here a continuous line of vocation from Isaiah's servant to Christ, to Paul and to all Christians. In his own mission to the nations, Paul says, after quoting Isaiah,

---

1 Kar Yong Lim, *The Sufferings of Christ are Abundant in Us: A Narrative Dynamics Investigation of Paul's Sufferings in 2 Corinthians* (London: T&T Clark International, 2009).

See, now is the acceptable time; see, now is the day of salvation! We are putting no obstacle in anyone's way, so that no fault may be found with our ministry, but as servants of God we have commended ourselves in every way: through great endurance, in afflictions, hardships, calamities, beatings imprisonments, riots, labours, sleepless nights, hunger; by purity, knowledge, patience, kindness, holiness of spirit, genuine love, truthful speech, and the power of God; with the weapons of righteousness for the right hand and for the left; in honour and dishonour, in ill repute and good repute. We are treated as impostors, and yet are true; as unknown, and yet are well known; as dying, and see – we are alive; as punished, and yet not killed; as sorrowful, yet always rejoicing; as poor, yet making many rich; as having nothing, and yet possessing everything. (2 Corinthians 6:2–10)

It is to this paradoxical lifestyle that people are called, for the central theme of Paul's letter is that God's power shows itself in transforming the lives of those whom the world regards as weak and inadequate.

Paul's attitude to suffering is quite different from that of Buddhism, for example, which also sees suffering at the heart of human existence but as an ineluctable condition of living in a transient, ever-changing world. The Buddhist's aim is to escape from existence in this world to reach an eternal nothingness where there can be no change or decay, no suffering and no God. Just nothing. Pope Benedict XVI was right to say that there is little in common between Christianity and Buddhism; they are two mutually opposed ways of making sense of the world. For Paul, suffering is a temporary penalty caused by living in a violent and loveless world. At its root is sin. He awaits Isaiah's 'day of salvation' when God will transform the world. In Christianity, in spite of present suffering, there is hope for something different, a new kind of existence, a truly human existence. Paul speaks of the peace he already has with God through Christ, and that

we boast in our hope of sharing the glory of God. And not only that, we also boast in our sufferings, knowing that suffering produces endurance, and endurance produces character, and character produces hope, and hope does not disappoint us, because God's love has been poured into our hearts through the Holy Spirit that has been given to us. (Romans 5:2–5)

He speaks of the 'privilege' one has of believing in Christ and suffering for him, and he invites his readers to share in his own struggle (Philippians 1:29). Sharing the sufferings and death of Christ makes one become like him, writes Paul, and so he endures this himself in order to attain the resurrection from the dead (Philippians 3:10).

Transformed in Hope

Paul had no illusions about what it is like to live in the world. He would certainly have endorsed the sentiments of the later prayer: 'to you do we cry, poor banished children of Eve, to you do we send up our mourning and weeping in this vale of tears.' To acknowledge that life is difficult at times for most people, and all the time for many people, is no more than realism. The world is a vale of tears and to think otherwise is ignorant and complacent. But if there were nothing to Christianity but suffering, one would have to be a masochist to join the church. What Paul offers is hope that the world will be changed.

Hope can sometimes seem a weak word. We may be asked if our team will win this weekend or if our illness will have gone by Monday, and we answer, 'I hope so.' This usage just indicates a positive way of looking at everyday things, perhaps mixed with some wishful thinking. Paul, however, gives hope a much stronger sense because he took the word from the Old Testament. In the Psalms we find many references to 'hope' (*elpis* in Paul's Greek version) as in 'I hope in his word'. The King James Bible, translating from the Hebrew, uses this language of hope, though more recent versions prefer to speak of belief or trust, for what Paul found in the Old Testament was a concept that is virtually identical with 'faith' (*pistis*) and that involves total reliance on God. It is this trust or hope that determines how one lives one's life. Without it we may as well eat, drink and do whatever else makes you merry, for tomorrow we all die.[2] Paul assures us that suffering can be put to some purpose because we go from suffering, through endurance and character development to hope, and, Paul tells us, hope does not disappoint because the faithful have already received God's love through the Holy Spirit (Romans 5:3–5).

What is the content of this hope? Paul looks for a transformation of the very nature of our existence and, whatever form that might take, he calls it resurrection. It involves overcoming, not only present suffering, but death; and by death Paul means non-existence, nothingness, extinction – precisely the condition that Buddhism aspires to beyond a series of rebirths.

The language of resurrection is also derived from the Old Testament and originally it had nothing to do with dead individuals being brought back to life. It was about God being faithful to his covenant, vindicating Israel and restoring the fortunes of the nation. This is what Ezekiel 37 (the valley of bones) and Hosea 6:2 are about. The earliest references to God bringing back to life those who are literally dead are Isaiah 26:19 (thought to be a late addition to the eighth-century prophet), Daniel 12:2–3 and 2 Maccabees 7. All are from the second century BC. To this extent Christianity shares the same hope as late second-temple Judaism of a general resurrection that will accompany God's definitive judgement of the world. What changes this hope from being irrational wish-fulfilment to something that gives grounds for committing yourself to it is the resurrection of Jesus. The claim that resurrection has already happened to someone, in advance of the hoped-for general resurrection, first came in Jewish history from the followers of Jesus. If their claim turns out not to be true then, as Paul says, 'we are of all people most to be pitied' (1 Corinthians 15:19), because sin would still reign, there would be no compensation for the world's suffering, death as extinction would be our inexorable fate and there would be no point in looking for final meaning to our existence.

---

2   For the curious, the allusion is to 1 Cor. 15:32 where Paul cites Isa. 22:13 (there is an interpolation from Eccles. 8:15 in the popular saying that includes being merry), which is what the Israelites said when they were called to repentance. Much like modern times.

So resurrection is what Christian hope is about. What does Paul say about it? First, Paul had no direct experience of resurrection, so in one sense he does not know what he is talking about. If God did raise Jesus from the dead, the only one who experienced it was Jesus himself inside the tomb. So Paul bases everything he says on what he believes happened to Jesus and, as he cannot speak about it directly, he is forced to use metaphors to communicate the sense of what it might be about. His main point is that resurrection is more than a resuscitation back to life like that of Lazarus or someone who has had a near-death experience. It involves a transformation of our mode of existence:

> He will transform the body of our humiliation so that it may be conformed to the body of his glory, by the power that also enables him to make all things subject to himself. (Philippians 3:21)

When asked in 1 Corinthians 15 what the resurrection body will be like, Paul resorts to a pre-scientific biology, which is one of the things that makes the chapter difficult for us later readers. He suggests that in the animal world there are different kinds of flesh, which allows him to say that by analogy there can be such a thing as a glorified body as well as a natural body. And he resorts to a primitive astronomy to suggest that heavenly bodies – sun, moon, stars – have different levels of glory (does he mean brightness?), so a raised-up body can have a greater glory than our natural earthen body (15:39–41). He also turns to horticulture to show how, if you want a plant to grow, 'perhaps of wheat or of some other grain', you have to sow it (bury it, entomb it) and leave it alone and trust that it will eventually grow up into something new – as a seed becomes wheat or as an acorn becomes an oak tree (15:37f). He calls what has grown up a new kind of body.

After these various analogies, Paul says that what is sown, or in our case buried, is perishable, dishonourable, weak, an en-souled body; while what is raised (by God) is imperishable, glorious, full of power, and an en-spirited body (15:42–44).[3] What is important here is not to worry what Paul might mean by weak/powerful, dishonourable/glorious, en-souled/en-spirited for his point is the contrast between now and then when all will be *transformed*. We note that later in the chapter he adds mortal/immortal to perishable/imperishable (15:53f). In his earliest letter Paul surrounds the occasion with some vivid imagery: at Christ's command, with the archangel's call and the sound of God's trumpet (the *tuba mirum spargens sonum* from the *Dies Irae* of the Requiem Mass), the dead will rise from their graves, and we will meet the Lord in the air and be taken up into the clouds of heaven (1 Thessalonians 4:15–17). That this is no more than poetic imagery is clear from 1 Corinthians 15, written four or five years later, where only the image of the last trumpet has survived, and clearly even that should not be taken literally. The reality is unfathomable, what Paul calls a 'mystery'. The point is that 'we will all be changed, in a moment, in the twinkling of an eye' and so Paul announces that the reign of sin and death is over.

Paul believes all this, but on what basis does he hold it to be true? Everything he asserts comes from his knowledge of what happened to Jesus after his death and burial. His knowledge in the first place came from his encounter with the risen Christ, as Paul himself called it, on the Damascus road. We have three accounts of what happened, each slightly different in detail, and all come from Luke (Acts 9:1–9; 22:6–11; 26:12–16). Paul never described the event himself but he alludes to it in several places, notably in 1 Corinthians

---

3 Whenever Paul talks about us in this life and in the next, he consistently talks about our bodies. We are and shall continue to be bodily beings. But English translations of 1 Corinthians 15 usually give a misleading sense of the contrast between bodies as they are now and bodies to come. The NRSV is typical in saying 'It is sown a physical body, it is raised a spiritual body', as though Paul was emphasising a contrast between the physical and the spiritual and inadvertently allowing readers to skate over the word 'body'. So a common reading is to think that Paul says we now have a physical body but we will become spiritual. This is a misunderstanding. What Paul does is to distinguish the *sōma psuchikon* (a body deriving its life from *psuchē* or soul) from, at the resurrection, a *sōma pneumatikon* (a body getting its life from *pneuma* or spirit). For a lengthier discussion see N. T. Wright, *The Resurrection of the Son of God* (London: SPCK, 2003), pp. 348–53.

15:8 where he refers to himself being the last in a line of those who had seen the risen Christ, including five hundred at once in addition to the usual suspects. Who did he get this list from? Presumably from Peter and James when he met them in Jerusalem three years after his own experience on the road (Galatians 1:18f) – what else would they have talked about in the two weeks that Paul was with them?

So Paul's hope for release from the harsh realities of his daily existence and the prospect of final extinction, as well as the driving force behind his life as an apostle has content – it is what he calls resurrection – and it is grounded in what he is convinced happened to Jesus. There is, however, more to be said about Paul's hope than it being the expectation of some extraordinary divine event, over in a moment, in which the world is judged and those faithful to Christ will be vindicated with eternal life.

New Creation

Resurrection is about the fate of people, Jesus first and the rest later. The two Greek verbs used in the New Testament for being raised are very ordinary (*egeirō, anistēmi*) and just mean to get up or to arise, including the idea of getting up from bed in the morning. So the metaphor Paul uses is of people being woken up from the sleep of death. We awake refreshed and Paul stretches the metaphor to include this idea of transformation, not only of humanity but, in a daring passage in Romans 8:18–25, of the whole of creation. Creation is to be renewed.

Paul uses the expression 'new creation' in just two places: Galatians 6:15 and 2 Corinthians 5:17. The latter is the most interesting for us because it is about bodily existence and comes at the end of a long and complex argument. Paul writes, 'So if anyone is in Christ, there is a new creation: everything old has passed away; see, everything has become new.' Many commentators give this an individualist twist by asserting that the new creation comes with individual conversion and is to be associated with coming to faith in Christ and anticipating the age to come. New creation is an expression derived from the Old Testament, from Genesis 1—2 of course and from Isaiah 65:17 ('For I am about to create new heavens and a new earth'), and so is unlikely to have an individualistic meaning. It is about creation, all of it.

There is also a difficulty with translating Paul. His writing is very succinct; he just says, *hōste ei tis en Christō, kainē ktisis*, literally: 'so if anyone [is] in Christ, new creation'. This has led most translators to add some words to 'new creation' and what is added depends on how the expression is understood. C. K. Barrett has, 'if anyone is in Christ, *there is a* new *act of* creation.'[4] The RSV has, 'if anyone is in Christ, *he is a* new creation.' Because NRSV does not like gender-specific language, it modifies this to, 'if anyone is in Christ, *there is a* new creation.' Tom Wright plays safe and leaves it as it is and just writes, 'new creation'. Paul's language is the same in Galatians 6:15, though in a different context: 'For neither circumcision nor uncircumcision is anything, but new creation'. (NRSV has 'but a new creation is everything'.) It is not clear from Paul's own language in these two places whether the new creation is for people or for the whole of creation but, if we trace his argument carefully in 2 Corinthians 3—5, we can show it is the latter.

The context for 2 Corinthians 5:17 is the problem of living as a physical, material, natural body, which is contrasted with some sort of transformed, heavenly life. To understand how Paul got to this point we have to go back to chapter 3, perhaps the most anti-synagogue-Jewish passage in all his letters. The theme here is that of a new covenant. He announces that we have been made competent to be 'ministers of a new covenant, not of letter but of spirit; for the letter kills but the spirit gives life' (3:6). The old covenant was a covenant leading to death, chiselled on stone tablets. That covenant came in glory but it has faded, just as the glory of God which shone from Moses' face quickly faded (an allusion to Exodus 34:29–35). Paul then interprets Exodus in a preposterous way. The obvious meaning is that the Israelites could not look on Moses' face because they were blinded by the glory of God reflected in his face – a sort of divine radiation – so they put a veil over his face. However, Paul says that Moses veiled his own face to protect the Israelites from seeing that the glory of the Sinai covenant was already fading. He contrasts this covenant-of-fading-glory with the new spiritual covenant. He

---

4   C. K. Barrett, *A Commentary on the Second Epistle to the Corinthians* (London: Adam & Charles Black, 1973), pp. 162 and 173.

says that the minds of the followers of Moses and the law are still veiled when they read scripture, but when one turns to the Lord, the veil is removed (3:15f). 'And all of us, with unveiled faces, seeing the glory of the Lord ... are being transformed into the same image from one degree of glory to another' (3–18). The Lord, the *kurios* of the Old Testament, is now Jesus, of course. Where do we see the glory of the Lord? Paul says that God 'has shone in our hearts to give the light of the knowledge of the glory of God in the face of Jesus Christ' (4.6). We see God in the face of the man Jesus Christ and this transforms us, not only morally but substantially, ontologically if you like, in our very being.

However, we have this treasure in clay jars to show that the transformation comes from God and not from our own efforts. Meanwhile, we are afflicted but not crushed, perplexed but not driven to despair, persecuted but not forsaken, struck down but not destroyed (4:7–9). Paul says that we carry the death of Jesus in our bodies so that his life may also be made visible 'in our mortal flesh' (4:11). Our suffering in life reflects the manner of Jesus' death. But we also 'know that the one who raised the Lord Jesus will raise us also with Jesus and will bring us with you into his presence' (4:14). This clearly parallels 1 Corinthians 15:44 where Paul says that our 'natural body' (*soma psuchikon*, a body given life by the soul) will be transformed into a 'spiritual body' (*soma pneumatikon*, a body given life by the spirit). Paul is looking forward to a moment of eschatological transformation. This is confirmed by the final verses of chapter 4 of 2 Corinthians:

> So we do not lose heart. Even though our outer nature is wasting away, our inner nature is being renewed day by day. For this slight momentary affliction is preparing us for an eternal weight of glory beyond all measure, because we look not at what can be seen but at what cannot be seen; for what can be seen is temporary, but what cannot be seen is eternal. (4:16–18)

As we go into chapter 5, Paul says that if this 'earthly tent' is destroyed, as we can expect it to be, we have an eternal house from God in the heavens. As long as we are in this tent/body we *groan* under our present burden (5:4), we *groan* as we long for the heavenly dwelling (5:2) that God has prepared us for (5:5). Meanwhile our aim is to please the Lord (that is, Jesus Christ) for we shall appear before his judgement seat to give an account of what we have done in the body (5:6–10). Finally Paul adds:

> For the love of Christ urges us on, because we are convinced that one has died for all ... so that those who live might live no longer for themselves, but for him who died and was raised for them. From now on, therefore, we regard no one from a human point of view ... So if anyone is in Christ, new creation: everything old has passed away; see, everything has become new! (2 Corinthians 5:14–17)

Paul has a continuous line of argument from the first appearance of Moses with a veiled face, through looking on the glory of God in the face of Christ, a glory we hold in our earthen body, which is about to be transformed into a heavenly body, because we are already part of a new creation.

This leads us to Romans 8:18–25 and the reason for moving there is Paul's use of the verb *stenazō*, to groan, twice at 2 Corinthians 5:2 and 4, and twice at Romans 8:22 and 23. This remarkable passage is about the whole of creation with not a trace of individualism.

> I consider that the sufferings of this present time are not worth comparing with the glory about to be revealed to us. For creation waits with eager longing for the revealing of the children of God; for creation was subjected to futility, not of its own will but by the will of the one who subjected it, in hope that creation itself will be set free from its bondage to decay and will obtain the freedom of the glory of the children of God. We know that the whole of creation has been groaning together (*sustenazei*) and feeling the pains of child-birth (*sunōdinei*) until now; and not only creation but we ourselves, who have the first fruits of the Spirit, groan among ourselves (*en heautois stenazomen*) while we wait for adoption, the redemption of our bodies. (Romans 8:18–23 [in a slightly more literal version than NRSV])

This Romans passage – written slightly later than 2 Corinthians – is an extrapolation of 2 Corinthians 5 with its reference to new creation or the renewal of creation. In both places Paul refers to the transformation or redemption of our bodies into something to do with the Spirit, something heavenly. In our present condition, at the present time, we groan and suffer birth pangs while we wait for the completion of the transformation. Second Corinthians 5 focuses on people, but in Romans Paul explicitly brings the whole of creation into it. In this letter the transformation is no longer just of natural, earthen, human bodies but of everything natural and earthen. Presumably this includes not just living things but the inanimate earth too. Creation is said to be 'waiting with eager longing'; currently in a state of 'futility', because of its 'bondage to decay'. In these respects it is just like humanity. While Paul says that we wait for adoption and the redemption of our bodies, he also thinks that non-human creation is waiting for release from its 'bondage to decay' to share the freedom of the children of God. This is about God's transforming ownership and the revealing of creation's divine destiny – or however you think it should be expressed. What an extraordinary vision!

Romans 8:18–23 takes us through four stages:

1 the state of creation now – futile, decaying, groaning, but longing for the revealing of the children of God;
2 the state of us now – 'not only creation [groans] but we ourselves who have the first fruits of the Spirit';
3 our future status – adopted as children with redeemed bodies, as in 2 Corinthians 5; and raised up as in 1 Corinthians 15;
4 creation's future status – free from the bondage to decay, having obtained the freedom of the glory of the children of God.

Paul's comments on creation's future status then lead him to thoughts about hope (8:24–25). This passage makes it clear why in Romans 8:39 Paul thinks that 'nothing in the whole of creation will be able to separate us from the love of God in Christ Jesus our Lord' because in his vision all creation is to be transformed or renewed with us. This is a complex pattern of thought but it shows that Paul was a consistent and coherent thinker across different letters.

Christ is shown to be at the centre of creation in the cosmic psalm that Paul uses at Colossians 1:15–20, where he is said to be the firstborn of all creation; all things were created through him and all things are reconciled to him through the cross. This way of seeing Christ eventually leads to the Book of Revelation with its vision of a new earth and a new heaven, when the holy city, Jerusalem, will descend from heaven and God will dwell with his people. Then,

> Death will be no more, mourning and crying and pain will be no more, for the first things have passed away. And the one who was seated on the throne said, 'See, I am making all things new.' (Revelation 21:4–5)

This glances back to the prophecy, now about to be fulfilled, of Isaiah 65:17 and 66:22, but surely there is also an echo of 2 Corinthians 5:17: 'everything old has passed away; see, everything has become new.'

This is the hope to which all are called (Ephesians 1:18), the hope which makes the grieving of the bereaved only transitory (1 Thessalonians 4:13). Romans 13:11–14 makes it clear that the expectation that God will transform us and our world also makes a difference to how we live our lives now – not in debauchery and licentiousness, not in quarrelling and jealousy. But for the moment Paul leaves us with this blessing: 'May the God of hope fill you with all joy and peace in believing, so that you may abound in hope by the power of the Holy Spirit' (Romans 15:13).

7

Love

Love and the Old Testament

> And now faith, hope and love abide, these three; and the greatest of these is love. (1 Corinthians 13:13)

This triad of concepts appears in three other places in Paul: Colossians 1:4f ('for we have heard of your faith in Christ Jesus and of the love that you have for all the saints, because of the hope laid up for you in heaven'); 1 Thessalonians 1:3 ('remembering before our God and Father your work of faith and labour of love and steadfastness of hope in our Lord Jesus Christ'); and with some additional military imagery 1 Thessalonians 5:8 ('let us be sober, and put on the breastplate of faith and love, and for a helmet the hope of salvation'). This pattern suggests that Paul might have inherited the idea from an already existing pool of Christian rhetoric. Usually love comes second on the list suggesting a chronological pattern of coming to faith, living in love and hoping for future salvation, but in the famous poem of 1 Corinthians 13 Paul tells us that the greatest is love. In fact all three are bound together. We have already seen how, in some contexts in the Old Testament, faith and hope can be virtually equivalent, where 'hoping in God' is an expression of faith. Love might not be equivalent to faith or hope, but at the same time it is no more free-standing than is faith or hope. The kind of love that Paul outlines uses faith and hope as its foundation, while faith and hope are nothing without their practical expression in love.

Once more Paul's language and ideas are grounded in the Old Testament. The language of love is to be found all over the Jewish Bible, notably in the commandment against idolatry ('showing steadfast love to the thousandth generation of those who love me and keep my commandments', Exodus 20:6) and the daily prayer of Deuteronomy 6:4, 'Hear, O Israel: the Lord is our God, the Lord alone. You shall love the Lord your God with all your heart, and with all your soul, and with all your might.' The normal word for love in the Hebrew Old Testament, *'ahebh*, has a wide range of meaning. Apart from God's love and our love for God, it also covers the relation between a husband and wife, parents and children, the affection and loyalty of friends, as well as a devotion to righteousness. In the Septuagint it was translated by the Greek *agapē*. This was a happy choice for the earliest Christian writers. Outside the Septuagint and Jewish writings in Greek, *agapē* was hardly used before the Christian era. Greek had two other words for love: *erōs*, which referred to passionate, sexual love, and the more common *philia*, which could refer to the affection of friends, loyalty to the emperor and homeland or, more strongly, to the ties between parents and children. We should not tie down the meanings of these three Greek words too tightly as there are areas of overlap, but *erōs* is clearly not a suitable word for the love of God or Christians' love of each other and there is no use of *erōs* in the New Testament. And *philia* might be thought too soft a word in some contexts. So *agapē* it, fairly consistently, is – in the Gospels, in Paul and in John.

Love is mentioned in every one of Paul's letters and it is the bedrock of Christian ethics. Unlike some other forms of morality which centre on honour (one's own or one's family's) or pleasure or utility or self-interest or the acquisition of wealth or power, the Christian life, though disrupted by sin, is to be one of disinterested love – *agapē*. The pattern was set by Jesus but he had himself developed it from Jewish religion and its scriptures. The development of ethics in early Judaism was admirable and, with its monotheism, was the main reason why some Gentiles attached themselves to the synagogue as 'god-fearers', a group that provided many of the first converts to Christianity, which they would have seen as a 'gentilised' form of Judaism. Yet there was a limitation to Jewish moral law: it was not universal – it was a law for the Jews. For example, the commandment not to murder clearly did not cover killing foreigners because a lot of just such killing is recorded in Old Testament narratives and it is praised (see Psalm 149). After all it is in

Joshua, Judges and 1 Samuel that we find the first justification for Holy War, and with that went the killing of civilians and what we would now call ethnic cleansing. The commandment not to murder was seen only as a prohibition against taking the law into your own hands against other Jews. It was a prohibition of private vengeance. Holy War actually demanded murder and pillage against one's enemies. The driving force behind Old Testament ethics was the need to preserve God's holy community established by a covenant, and some of the laws that were designed to protect that community from its enemies can now look very harsh.

Yet Jewish ethics was not by any means static. It was repeatedly adapted to new historical circumstances, though the rules that had worked in earlier situations remained preserved in the written tradition alongside the new laws. This ethics also contains an element of pluralism, reflecting differences of opinion. Nor should one think that everything in Jewish tradition is legalistic, for there is visionary material in the Jewish Bible, which portrays an ideal moral community in which the lion will lie down with the lamb and there will be no more violence or war. There are even some hints of universalism, in Isaiah for example, but a turning point came with Jesus who universalised the morality of early Judaism. We must love God (Deuteronomy 6:5) and our neighbour (Leviticus 19:18), and when asked who our neighbour is Jesus told the tale of the Good Samaritan (Luke 10:29–37). There is no evidence that Jesus went out of his way to positively attract non-Jews but when they came to him they met no resistance. In the Sermon on the Mount Jesus tells his audience that they must love not only their friends ('do not even the tax-collectors and Gentiles do the same?') but also their enemies and even those who persecute them (Matthew 5:43–47; cf. Luke 6:32ff). When it comes to *agapē*, there are no limits.

Love comes from the Father–Son–Spirit

This is the teaching that Paul received from the apostles before him and the tradition that he continued. As you would expect, the first sense of love/*agapē* is the love believers should show to each other. Paul says little or nothing about the love Christians might show to those outside their communities, though some of his general statements such as 1 Corinthians 13 might be seen to have such wide-ranging implications. That he said little about outsiders is surely because of the context of his writings – he was writing *letters* to other Christian believers. Nonetheless, he fits his interest in the practice of love in his Christian communities into a wider theological framework.

In Paul's theological account of love, first place is given to God's own love which he shows through his Son, but the Father and Son are so closely bound together by Paul that divine love seems to have a single origin (2 Thessalonians 2:16). He speaks of 'the love of God in Christ Jesus our Lord' (Romans 8:39). God's love shows itself through the cross: 'God proves his love for us in that while we were still sinners Christ died for us' (Romans 5:8). The idea that love has its origin in a death is a harsh doctrine at the centre of Paul's thought. There is nothing sentimental about love; love shows itself in torture and execution. And this love is an act of generosity towards those, 'sinners', who have done nothing to deserve it. 'He has rescued us from the power of darkness and transferred us into the kingdom of his beloved Son, in whom we have redemption, the forgiveness of sins' (Colossians 1:13).

In the jubilant close of his long argument in Romans 8 about our transference from death to life, Paul asks who can be against us if God is for us (8:31) and he asserts that nothing can now separate us from the love of Christ (8:35, 39) for 'we are more than conquerors through him who loved us' (8:37). Who is the 'him who loved us'? It could be the Father or the Son. For Paul it looks as though it can be both. In Ephesians we have to imitate God as children loved by the Father, *and* we have to live in love just as Christ loved us (Ephesians 5:2). While it is God the Father who initiates the bringing of love back into a loveless world, the pattern for what that love might be is laid down by the Son. And from this Paul looks to a future where he might attain his own final transformation in the resurrection, the prize of our having been called by God, 'because Christ has made me his own' (Philippians 3:12ff). Love, then, has its origin in both Father and Son.

God's love is not only out there, so to speak, on public display on the cross and at the resurrection of his Son. There is also an experiential side to God's love and it has a Trinitarian pattern because the Spirit comes into it too: 'God's love has been poured into our hearts through the Holy Spirit that has been given to us' (Romans 5:5). In one of his virtue lists, Paul characterises love as one of the fruits of the Spirit (Galatians 5:22; see also Colossians 1:8). So there we have it: Father, Son and Spirit. This may not yet have the schematic form that it was to receive in the fourth-century Trinitarian creeds of Nicaea and Constantinople but, even at this early time when Paul was making theological sense of the Christian life, he was working within an incarnational and Trinitarian pattern. This theological pattern was to show that while the initiative comes from God, the purpose – and it is the purpose of *God* – is to turn *people*, all people, into loving creatures. So Paul says we have to love God (Romans 8:28; 1 Corinthians 8:3) (by which he means the whole Godhead) and we have to extend that to love one another (2 Thessalonians 1:3; Colossians 3:14). Several times Paul expresses his love for those to whom he was writing (1 Corinthians 16:24; 2 Corinthians 2:4). In Philippians he urges his readers to be of one mind with him and with Christ and, while we have seen in Chapter 2 that this is humble-mindedness, it is rooted in love:

> If then there is any encouragement in Christ, any consolation from love, any sharing in the Spirit, any compassion and sympathy, make my joy complete: be of the same mind, having the same love, being in full accord and of one mind. (Philippians 2:1–2).

This shared love is primarily concerned with seeking the interests of others rather than one's own and leads to humility. *Agapē* is the disinterested love of others, yet when he addressed his readers as 'beloved' he is not so much expressing his own love for them as telling them that they are loved by God.

John's Account of Love

The sequence we have found in Paul of grounding the love that Christians must show among each other in the love we have seen in Christ, and which is in turn grounded in the love that comes from God the Father, was developed more clearly and systematically at a slightly later date by John. First, the love that comes from God. This is summed up in John 3:16, the text that is placarded by evangelical supporters in athletics stadiums around the world:

> For God so loved the world that he gave his only Son, so that everyone who believes in him may not perish but may have eternal life.

We find the threefold pattern of 3:16 (i.e. Father, Son and everyone who believes) repeated in Jesus' long final prayer in John's Gospel which emphasises the unity of Father, Son and the disciples 'so that the world may know that you have sent me and have loved them even as you have loved me' (17:23). Christ's love is directed towards the Father (14:31) and towards his disciples (13:1) who will in turn be loved by the Father (14:21). The love of the Father and the Son is then to be taken up and practised by Christ's followers. His commandment, the 'new commandment' that encapsulates all others, is that they love each another: 'Just as I have loved you, you also should love one another' (13:34; 15:12f). Laying down your life for your friends is said to be the act of greatest love, where 'taking up your cross' can be taken to its limit. Again we have a pattern of imitation where all are not only of one mind but of one action.

> Those who love me will keep my word, and my Father will love them, and we will come to them and make our home with them. Whoever does not love me does not keep my words; and the word that you hear is not mine, but is from the Father who sent me. (14:23f)

The sequence in John, as in Paul, is Father–Son–disciples. In a nutshell: 'As the Father loved me, so I have loved you; abide in my love' (15:9; 17:26).

The same scheme is to be found in the First Letter of John which is dominated even more by the theme of love than are the final discourses that Jesus has with his disciples in the Fourth Gospel (chapters 13—16). John's readers are called children of God because of the love that comes from the Father (1 John 3:1; 4:16). They know what love is by looking at the example of Jesus who laid down his life for us, something they also may be called to do (4:16). In fact the author of this letter speaks much more about the love of God than of Christ but this is because the author clearly believes that Jesus Christ is God incarnate, God in the flesh. We see this explicitly in the introduction to the Gospel (1:1–18) but also, in case you think the Gospel and the Letters come from different authors, at 1 John 2:22f and 2 John 7. It is well known that John has a high Christology – that is, that Jesus the Christ/Messiah is in some sense divine, a representation, an incarnation of God the creator – but Paul holds the Father and Son together just as closely, as we shall see later.

The author of the letters is particularly concerned about the behaviour of his readers and that is because of the historical context of the community to whom he was writing. The letters come from close to the end of the first century and were written for what had become a divided community. Someone whom the author calls the antichrist, together with other 'deceivers', has formed a splinter group that denies the incarnation of Jesus. While John thinks it important to have correct beliefs about Jesus as God-in-the-flesh, he is also concerned about the behaviour of those to whom he writes because he says that no one can claim to love God and hate his brothers and sisters. If they do not love each other whom they can see, they cannot be said to love God whom they cannot see. John is not actually anxious about their behaviour but he emphasises that it is love that should distinguish them from those who have left the community to follow whoever is the antichrist. Loving one's brothers and sisters is what should mark out those who live the Christian life. The whole of 1 John is in effect a meditation on the nature of Christian love, especially chapters 3 and 4, and particularly 4:7–12 and 16–21.

> God is love, and those who abide in love abide in God, and God abides in them. Love has been perfected among us in this: that we may have boldness on the day of judgement, because as he is, so are we in this world. There is no fear in love, but perfect love casts out fear; for fear has to do with punishment, and whoever fears has not reached perfection in love. We love because he first loved us. Those who say, 'I love God,' and hate their brothers or sisters, are liars; for those who do not love a brother or sister whom they have seen, cannot

love God whom they have not seen. The commandment we have from him is this: those who love God must love their brothers and sisters also. (1 John 4:16–21)

It may not be the whole truth to say that 'love is all you need' but it is not far off the mark. What the slogan may lack is a transcendental grounding.

Back to Paul

John has the virtue of having a clear theological plan for showing where our mutual love comes from, but after a time his rhetoric seems to be, not exactly vacuous, but lacking in specificity. The issue remains: what do we actually have to do, or not do? In this respect Paul is more exact than John and it may be because Paul had more awkward issues to deal with in his churches than John. He wrote to the Galatians about their new-found freedom and told them they were no longer under the law (Galatians 5:1, 13, 18 and 23). When taken out of context, and apart from whatever Paul might have *said* to his churches that has not been written down, this argument led some of his readers to think that because they were no longer under the law, they could do as they liked. This sounds suspiciously like a few opportunists taking advantage of a message of relative freedom designed for those law-loving Galatians who were unreasonably strict. Even so, it is possible to understand the commandment to love in such a way as to allow all kinds of self-indulgence that Paul would not have approved of. He deals with this at the opening of Romans 6, where he imagines his readers asking him rhetorically whether we should remain in sin so that grace might abound. This seems an odd idea to have to refute. The idea seems to be that, according to Paul's theology, God is so generous with his love that he will forgive all who turn to him – they are justified before God by their faith. God's job, his raison d'être, so to speak, is to hand out grace. The more sinful people are in the world, the more God will be able to show how gracious he is. So if we continue to live sinful lives, the more we will help God to be true to his own nature, that of gracefully forgiving sinners. This is a neat argument: to suggest that the more dissolute we are, the more we are doing God a favour. But did any Christians in Rome actually believe this?

Paul's first attempt to respond to this strange argument alludes to our having died a spiritual death at baptism in order to live a new life with the promise of resurrection (Romans 6:1–11). Here his argument is about our identification in baptism with Christ, who has overcome sin and death. Then at 6:15 he asks a second rhetorical question similar to the first at 6:1: 'Should we sin because we are not under law but under grace?' His response to this is to tie sin and death together to show that you cannot have the one without the other, 'for the wages of sin is death' (6:16–23). If you persist in sin, you die. So the obedience of faith, then, does not mean persisting in sin and lawlessness. Paul follows the example of Jesus' twofold commandment to love God and your neighbour. He tells us that the whole of the law is summed up in the single commandment to love your neighbour (Galatians 5:14), and again to 'owe no one anything, except to love one another; for the one who loves another fulfils the law' (Romans 13:8). But still there remains the question of whether the commandment to love has much specific content, in spite of the brief list of commandments that Paul alludes to at this point in Romans 13.

Augustine famously said that we should love and do as we will. This might suggest that there are no rules at all for us to follow other than to love. In the 1960s there was a style of Christian ethics called Situation Ethics that had some popularity at the time. It was started by an American, Joseph Fletcher, and quickly found a place on examination syllabuses. Fletcher found his inspiration in Augustine and claimed that a Christian has to be a loving person but beyond that there are no absolute moral rules that cover all cases and that allow for no exceptions, no matter what the circumstances. According to Fletcher we must always do what we consider to be the loving thing, but beyond that we have to decide for ourselves what it might be in the situation in which we find ourselves; hence, situation ethics. This is a moral position that is not far removed from relativism, but while relativism (a defining characteristic of what has come to be known as postmodernism[1]) abandons all moral rules on the grounds that moral codes are only cultural products from

---

1   See E. Gellner. *Postmodernism, Reason and Religion* (London: Routledge, 1992).

different societies (so that what a person thinks is right is relative to the society he comes from), situation ethics holds one basic presupposition: that we should always take the most loving option. One example of how this can work which some seem to find attractive is to say that as there are no absolute moral rules, there is no rule that 'we should never take innocent human life', a rule which could be applied to unwanted pregnancies, childhood diseases, euthanasia and care of the elderly. Situation Ethics asks us to work out in each individual situation what it would be to love our neighbour, for there are no rules to guide our decisions. In one case it might mean preserving a life, in another case it might mean ending a life. We decide according to the circumstances; no rules. So it is not the case that anything goes in Situation Ethics, but it does leave a lot of freedom for the individual conscience.

The limitation of this form of ethics has been made clear by Herbert McCabe, who argues in *Law, Love and Language* (1968) that there are actions which of themselves are incompatible with being loving. If it were not so and, depending on the situation, *any* action *could* be loving, then the concept would be vacuous – it would not tell us anything about 'love'. And there are actions that could never be loving no matter what the situation: killing babies, starving the poor, gassing Jews for example. So there *are* cases where we *can* frame absolute moral rules, i.e., rules that are independent of circumstances. It may turn out that there are only a limited number of such rules, but as a friend once said: students are almost always moral relativists until you ask them whether they think paedophilia is acceptable. Timothy Radcliffe has suggested that paedophilia has become in our society the only sexual sin – he might add rape to his list.[2] However, our question here is whether Paul, in his disquisition on love, gives any support to those who are sympathetic to Situation Ethics. Now that we are free of the law, does Paul give much content to his recommendation that we should love one another?

Paul expected moral maturity in his readers and he shows some sympathy for an ethics that does not require rules. He tells the Christians in Thessalonica that he does not need to write to them

---

2   Timothy Radcliffe, *The Tablet*, 19/26 (December 2009), p. 13.

about loving their brothers and sisters because they have been taught by God to love one another (1 Thessalonians 4:9). They know what it is all about so they do not need a written code. It is, one might say, on their hearts and in their minds. They may be encouraged to act spontaneously and may normally count on doing the right thing.

Some years ago I worked in a secondary school in England that prided itself, and exasperated some of the more conventional local people outside the school, that it had no school rules. At any rate there was no code that could be produced for pupils or their parents. This contrasted with one independent boarding school I had reason to visit some years ago that published their many rules on a board in the corridor. These included complex arrangements about which master was deputed to give permission to which pupils for a visit to the local town, as well as the explicit instruction that no pupil should bring firearms or explosives into the school. Did they need to be told? I suppose it was to stop them bringing daddy's shotgun on to the premises.[3] My school, however, did have one rule: pupils should look after each other. To take one example of how this worked, pupils were urged to tell *someone* if they saw bullying taking place – this is always a problem because pupils are bullied into sharing a culture of not ratting on the bullies. But this school took bullying very seriously and, so far as one could tell, it was very uncommon in the school. If someone did something wicked or dangerous, they were not excused by claiming there was no rule against it. They were expected to be mature enough to know what was expected of them. This school was not perfect but it had the best behaviour I have seen in any publicly funded school. So it is with Paul. In effect he says 'work it out for yourself': 'And this is my prayer, that your love may overflow more and more with knowledge and full insight to help you to determine what is best' (Philippians 1:9f). Paul is able to give content to the command to love but, as we have seen, he rarely does it in the form of specific rules. To the Galatians he says, 'Bear one another's burdens, and in this way you will fulfil the law of Christ' (Galatians 6:2). This is rather like the school rule that pupils should support each other.

---

3 I did once work in a school where a pupil turned up with a shotgun (unloaded) but that is another story.

Yet there *is* content to Paul's loving. In Romans he speaks of love fulfilling the law and he refers on this occasion to specific commandments: not to commit adultery, murder, steal or covet and to do no wrong to your neighbour (Romans 13:8–10). He can't cover every example of good behaviour so he normally gives a generalised account of what love involves, as in this extended passage from Romans:

> Let love be genuine; hate what is evil, hold fast to what is good; love one another with mutual affection; outdo one another in showing honour. Do not lag in zeal, be ardent in spirit, serve the Lord. Rejoice in hope, be patient in suffering, persevere in prayer. Contribute to the needs of the saints; extend hospitality to strangers. Bless those who persecute you; bless and do not curse them. Rejoice with those who rejoice, weep with those who weep. Live in harmony with one another; do not be haughty, but associate with the lowly; do not claim to be wiser than you are. Do not repay anyone evil for evil, but take thought for what is noble in the sight of all. If it is possible, so far as it depends on you, live peaceably with all. (Romans 12:9–18)

To the Corinthians he says that love means gentleness (1 Corinthians 4:21). All this without having yet referred, as we should now do, to Paul's celebrated poem in 1 Corinthians 13 where he tells us that:

> Love is patient; love is kind; love is not envious or boastful or arrogant or rude. It does not insist on its own way; it is not irritable or resentful; it does not rejoice in wrongdoing, but rejoices in the truth. It bears all things, believes all things [or better: is faithful in all things], hopes all things, endures all things. (1 Corinthians 13:4–7)

Here is firm content for what love means. And at this point one can see why this passage is such a popular reading at weddings, though its original context has nothing directly to do with marriage at all. In 1 Corinthians Paul praises love alongside the gifts of the Spirit, which he discusses immediately before and after chapter 13, but more on that discussion later.

Now we can see how appropriate it is for Paul to frame his ethics around the idea that in order to develop our moral character we must expunge vices and cultivate virtues. This is the idea that we discussed in Chapter 1, that Paul's ethics is about character, not law, and that Paul preferred to list vices and virtues in place of traditional codes of practice. The problem with people who live by rules is that they are in danger of doing only what the rules require and never stepping imaginatively beyond them. The morally immature think that if some act is not explicitly prohibited by a law, then it is permitted. In reality most of our faults are sins of omission – not the breaking of rules, but failing to do what we should through weakness, cowardice or embarrassment. The mature take charge of their lives and start behaving creatively, imaginatively and courageously. Rules are not always appropriate when trying to live a life of love towards others, provided you have good character. A generosity of spirit is required that leaves the rule-book behind.

As we have seen, Paul explicitly rejects the law, by which he means the Jewish Torah, but as his moral standards are both traditional and strict and also more demanding than ever, a debate has opened about how much of the Jewish law Paul actually wanted to reject. No one claims that Paul wanted to keep every legal requirement in the Torah; that would be to ignore his stance on the circumcision issue and would fly in the face of central parts of Romans and Galatians. At the other end of the spectrum we find the majority of Pauline scholars who have taken him literally and understood him to have rejected the whole of the Torah. Others maintain a middle position: that because Paul sticks by the *moral* requirements of the Jewish scriptures, his rejection of the law is limited to the *ritual* commandments: namely, the injunctions to circumcise, keep kosher and purity and the Sabbath,[4] and how to sacrifice. These 'boundary markers', as they have been called, are what distinguish Jews from others and draw a line between who is in

---

4 The first Christians quickly changed their day of observance to 'the Lord's day', i.e., the day of the resurrection.

their community and who is outside. For Paul, everyone can be in and boundary markers certainly have to go. Yet virtue may not here lie in the mean, and to work through the apparent contradictions, or at the least the tensions, that we find in Paul's letters, we surely have to look at things in a different perspective. There is a sense in which Paul keeps the law and another sense in which he rejects it. And whether he judges the law positively, as he does on the whole in Romans, or negatively, as in Galatians, depends on the social context of each letter. It depends on what he is writing about and to whom. It is not so much that Paul repudiates the law, but rather that he pushes it into the background and invites us to think about our moral lives in a different kind of way. Certainly the ritual commandments of the Torah and even some of its more bizarre moral commandments are inappropriate in the 'new age' in which Paul lives. In this new situation after Christ, his readers have to show some moral maturity and stop thinking like children (1 Corinthians 13:11).

Is it possible, then, to sum up simply what the Christian life is about? Paul does it admirably. While engaging in a dispute with those in Galatia about male Gentile converts, Paul insists that whether one is circumcised or not counts for nothing; the only thing that counts is 'faith working through love' (Galatians 5:6).

8

Holiness

Holiness in the Old Testament

'Holiness' is rooted, as much as any concept in this book, in the Old Testament. There is some dispute over whether the root meaning of the Hebrew *qādôš* has to do with the separateness of God from creation or whether it is to do with his 'brightness' or glory. The latter is probably the basic meaning, for God's holiness is in the first place about his power and majesty.

> The Lord is king; let the peoples tremble!
> He sits enthroned among the cherubim; let the earth quake!
> The Lord is great in Zion; he is exalted over all the peoples.
> Let them praise your great and awesome name. Holy is he!
> Mighty King, lover of justice, you have established equity;
>   you have executed justice and righteousness in Jacob.
> Extol the Lord our God; worship at his footstool.
> Holy is he! (Psalm 99:1–5)

'The Holy One of Israel', as Isaiah calls him, is the one who inspires fear, whom no man can approach: 'you cannot see my face, for no one shall see me and live' (Exodus 33:20). Yet it is precisely the immense power of God that makes God separate from creatures. While this places a great gulf between God and humankind, the primary sense is that because God is holy, God separates himself from *other gods*. So any person or object that is declared holy is to be kept separate from pagan religious activity and from anything that is declared secular or profane or unclean. God's having elected a people makes them holy because election draws them away from the

other nations who have other gods. The wish of the God of the Old
Testament for his people is that 'You shall be holy, for I the LORD
your God am holy' (Leviticus 19:2; see also 1 Peter 1:16). So the
Israelites are a holy people, who live in a holy land, with a holy city
at its centre – 'the place that the Lord your God will choose as a
dwelling for his name', as Deuteronomy puts it. It is clear from this
that holiness is not (yet) a moral quality but, rather like 'righteousness', it points to a relationship with God. To be holy is to be
brought into contact with the divine.

The religious practices of the Jewish cult were a public demon-
stration of the elect status of this people – holy and righteous before
God. However, in the Holiness Code of Leviticus (chapters
17—26) and in the speeches of Moses in Deuteronomy, moral
obligations are also seen to be placed on the people. Moses tells the
people to 'observe diligently all the words of this law'; to choose life
and so avoid God's punishment of wrath and death. Being holy,
then, involves becoming godlike, which entails developing a certain
moral character, exemplified in Deuteronomy by a strict and
explicit moral code.

It will be clear from our earlier discussion that Paul will not rely
on the law to bring holiness but is likely to see it grow hand in hand
with moral development cultivated by love. But for Paul there is a
major obstacle to this, and it is sin.

The Power of Sin

Sin is not exactly a popular idea these days, though its reality seems
to be as common as ever. The word is normally taken to refer to a
wrongful act. In that sense it is possible to multiply sins, count them
up and, if you are so inclined, confess that you have committed
perhaps 97 sins since breakfast. You might be offered the pastoral
advice to commit fewer (preferably none at all, but we are all
fallible). However, this is not Paul's prime understanding of the
word. His understanding is flexible; the word can have different
senses in different contexts. Sometimes, though not normally, he
uses the word in the plural, which does indeed have the sense that
sins are particular actions (e.g. 1 Thessalonians 2:16; Romans 3:25).
Elsewhere, when he speaks of you being 'in your sins' (1 Corinthi-

ans 15:17) he can point to a condition that you are in. While being made 'to be sin' (in this case, Christ) in 2 Corinthians 5:21 is the equivalent of 'being mortal'.

Paul's normal use refers to sin in the singular where it usually has the sense of being a force, a cosmic force, that can take people over so they are no longer in control of their own behaviour. He speaks of us being enslaved to sin. Paul has a lengthy meditation on sin in Romans 5—8, though it should not be thought that he was obsessed by sin, for the word turns up only infrequently elsewhere in his letters. There are 59 uses of 'sin' (*hamartia*) in Paul's authentic letters and 48 of these are in Romans, mainly in those central chapters 5—8. In chapter 5 he considers where sin came from and he relates its origin to Adam. As a Jew of the first century, Paul would have read Genesis 2—3 historically and literally and he would have seen Adam's original sin in the garden bringing death directly to the human race through God's punishment of the first couple, as indicated by Genesis 2:16–17 and 3:19. 'Just as sin came into the world through one man, and death came through sin, so death spread to all because all have sinned' (Romans 5:12). Sin and death are bound together here, as are righteousness, holiness and eternal life as their opposite elsewhere in Romans. The wages or reward for sin is death. As death is contrasted with eternal life, we can take it that death means eternal death. So, for Paul, death means destruction, nothingness, the end of it all – which is what the non-religious expect anyway. This is what the reign of sin leads to for everyone, Jew or Gentile (Romans 2:12; 3:9). And while everyone is subject to sin and has to die, it is only the righteous, the faithful ones, who will be raised to life.

In Paul's time, a common understanding for moral failure was the Socratic one that it was due to a person's lack of knowledge. This might be the result of a poor upbringing, inferior education or indolence later in life. To be good, a person was instructed to 'know yourself' and to learn the norms of good behaviour and how to apply them. This is the outlook you find among the Stoics in the first century and it has been suggested that Paul might have been influenced in some respects by the Stoics. For Epictetus, a Stoic philosopher who lived slightly later than Paul, the solution to bad behaviour was good education.[1] This is why the Stoics tolerated chattel slavery: only the educated could be free and trusted to behave well, while the common people needed to be placed under the rule of a master. The many (*hoi polloi*) were certainly not trusted with any democratic responsibility for the framing of legislation, especially as most of them were illiterate. The attraction of this explanation for immorality – lack of knowledge to be corrected by better education – is that it spurns any reference to what might be called the supernatural or the metaphysical. But Paul offers a quite different understanding in Romans 7:7–25. He thinks the problem is sin, and the solution to that is not better schooling.

At Romans 7:15 Paul portrays a man who is well educated by Stoic standards. He knows the law, which can mean any set of moral laws but for Paul it primarily meant the Torah. Yet this educated man finds himself doing what he knows he should not do and not doing what he knows he should. In his case, knowing the law does not help improve his behaviour, indeed it sometimes makes it worse. How can this be? The law is educative in the way it opens up intriguing new possibilities, things that one might not otherwise have thought of doing. Prohibitions exert their own fascination and our lower selves are drawn into finding what they forbid desirable. When schoolchildren are told not to smoke behind the bicycle sheds, that becomes exactly what they want to do. It may be perverse but that is how people behave. So, while the law tells us quite rightly what we should and should not do, in reality the law is a problem. It can actually lead us towards sin. Some people might want to say that the law is part of what sin is. However, that is not how Paul sees it. He refuses to say that the law is sin because it has come from God through Moses and it tells us objectively what is right and what is wrong. Nor does he even go so far as to say that the law leads us into sin. It is sin that draws us into wrongdoing, though there can be some unintended provocation from the law/Torah.

> I do not understand my own actions. For I do not do what I want, but I do the very thing I hate. Now if I do what I do

---

1 For example see Niko Huttunen, *Paul and Epictetus on Law: A Comparison* (London: T&T Clark, 2009), ch. 6.

not want, I agree that the law is good. But in fact it is no longer I that do it, but sin that dwells within me ... For I do not do the good I want, but the evil I do not want is what I do. Now if I do what I do not want, it is no longer I that do it, but sin that dwells within me. (Romans 7:15–20)

Paul is not here trying to evade moral responsibility, on the contrary he is portraying a man who is not in control of himself and this is because he is enslaved to sin.

So I find it to be a law that when I want to do what is good, evil lies close at hand. For I delight in the law of God in my inmost self, but I see in my members another law at war with the law of my mind, making me captive to the law of sin. (7:21–23)

Is this a common experience for the morally conscientious? Or were the Stoics right? Do we behave badly because we are ignorant of how to behave or because we are too weak to do what we know we should do? Only the reader can answer that, but it may be that Paul is more in touch with reality than the average educated Stoic.

The example Paul uses to illustrate this moral weakness is covetousness. This may seem to us a rather old-fashioned example, but not so. In the economically developed West, our modern consumer society thrives on coveting – 'pass me my credit card and lead me to those designer handbags.' For Paul, coveting would have meant any form of improper desire and in his time he would not have been interested in the narrower sense of consumer goods.[2] Paul presents his case in the first person.

What then should we say? That the law is sin? By no means! Yet, if it had not been for the law, I would not have known sin. I would not have known what it is to covet if the law had

---

2 *Epithumia* can sometimes mean legitimate desires but more often it refers to sinful desires generally, and coveting and lust more specifically – see J. D. G. Dunn, *The Theology of Paul the Apostle* (Edinburgh: T&T Clark, 1998), p. 120.

not said, 'You shall not covet.' But sin, seizing an opportunity in the commandment, produced in me all kinds of covetousness. Apart from the law sin lies dead. I was once alive apart from the law, but when the commandment came, sin revived and I died, and the very commandment that promised life proved to be death to me. For sin, seizing an opportunity in the commandment, deceived me and through it killed me. So the law is holy, and the commandment is holy and just and good. Did what is good, then, bring death to me? By no means! It was sin, working death in me through what is good, in order that sin might be shown to be sin, and through the commandment might become sinful beyond measure. For we know that the law is spiritual; but I am of the flesh, sold into slavery under sin. (7:7–14)

Paul then continues with the passage referred to above about not understanding his own actions (7:15–23).

Who is 'I' in Romans 7? Though the psychology of being under sin in vv. 15ff appears to come from his own experience, it cannot be Paul because Paul was never alive apart from the law, as in v. 9. James Dunn calls the 'I' 'adam' in the sense of 'everyman', which is about right. Sin came into the world (from the time of Adam) but 'I' was once alive apart from the law until the commandment came (with Moses), when sin revived and 'I' died. The law promised life but it did not deliver it. The law brought death because sin was stirred up and corrupted 'me' and made 'me' incapable of keeping the law (does Paul mean incapable of keeping it consistently, or incapable of keeping it at all?). Indeed the law provoked 'me' into breaking even more laws than 'I' would otherwise have done. It is clear in Paul's scheme of things that it will be impossible for 'me' to become good, moral, righteous, just or holy unless something is done about sin. This something will have to be more than a Stoic education, for the Torah is good enough as a moral educator. We are all locked into a moral imprisonment under law, sin and death, Paul says, and our release will have to come from a source that has the strength to destroy the power of sin. He announces this release at the end of the chapter: 'Wretched man that I am! Who will rescue me from this body of death? Thanks be to God through Jesus Christ our Lord!' (7.24f).

Life in the Flesh versus Life in the Spirit

First a brief note about another of Paul's expressions that points to the negative side of human life: 'in the flesh'. This can sometimes indicate the literal sense of flesh, meaning our bodiliness insofar as it is mortal, as in 'flesh and blood cannot inherit the kingdom of God' (1 Corinthians 15:50; see also 2 Corinthians 10:3; Galatians 2:20; Philippians 1:22, 24). The more interesting use, however, is of 'flesh' as a metaphor for life before baptism. Paul uses it four times in Romans 7 to point to a life enslaved to sin (7:5, 14, 18, 25). There is a similar use in chapter 8 where Paul wants to emphasise the transformation that comes with baptism, a transformation which has already taken place in the lives of his readers. His first uses of 'flesh' in this chapter refer to our mortality, while the later uses refer to a way of life.

> There is therefore now no condemnation for those who are in Christ Jesus. For the law of the spirit of life in Christ Jesus has set you free from the law of sin and of death. For God has done what the law, weakened by the flesh, could not do: by sending his own Son in the likeness of sinful flesh, and to deal with sin, he condemned sin in the flesh, so that the just requirement of the law might be fulfilled in us, who walk not according to the flesh but according to the spirit. For those who live according to the flesh set their minds on the things of the flesh, but those who live according to the spirit set their minds on the things of the spirit. To set the mind on the flesh is death, but to set the mind on the spirit is life and peace. (8:1–6)

Again we have the idea of 'mindedness' that we found in Philippians where it is humble-mindedness. In Romans 8, fleshly-mindedness is its opposite. Paul's use of 'flesh', then, has nothing particularly to do with sex – what some might call sins of the flesh. It is a metaphor for a life lived apart from and in hostility to God (8:7).

Paul contrasts flesh with spirit, so spirit points to the Christian life after baptism (in this context, contrary to the NRSV translation, it is better not to give 'spirit' an upper-case S). The word 'flesh' does not, then, lead us towards a Platonic dualism between conflicting worlds of matter and spirit, the kind of dualism that some Gnostics tried to bring into Christian belief in the second century and that John anticipated and opposed in his Gospel. Salvation does not consist in abandoning our physicality and all the things of this material world in order to be released into a divine, spiritual existence as the Gnostics thought. Nonetheless, Christian life certainly *is* a life in the Spirit. 'You are not in the flesh; you are in the Spirit, since the Spirit of God dwells in you' (Romans 8:9). Paul is also aware that a person's conversion is not always cut and dried in terms of spiritual regeneration. He told the Christians in Corinth that they were still people of the flesh rather than spiritual people. He calls them immature, to be fed on milk not solid food, and the sign of this is their jealousy and quarrelling (1 Corinthians 3:1–3). The Galatians were a problem for him too. He asks them if they had received the Spirit only to end with the flesh (Galatians 3:3). His argument with the Galatians centred on their surprising desire for circumcision, a matter of the flesh in more than one sense. It is in this letter that Paul created his celebrated allegory about the two wives of Abraham, Sarah and Hagar, and their children, Isaac and Ishmael. He tells us explicitly that this is an allegory about two covenants (Galatians 4:21–31). On the one side we have Hagar, the slave woman, whose child was born according to the flesh; she represents the Sinai covenant which corresponds to the earthly Jerusalem. On the other side we have Sarah, the free woman, whose son is born from God's promise, who is the representative of the heavenly Jerusalem, 'and she is our mother' (4:26). Here Paul tendentiously identifies the covenant of flesh (playing on the idea of circumcision) with the Judaism of the temple and synagogue, and its written law (compare 3:2f). By contrast Christians are identified with a spiritual covenant, recalling but not actually quoting Jeremiah (31:31–34). In a different context, Paul speaks of the written letter killing but the spirit giving life (2 Corinthians 3:6). Biographically, the radical change in Paul's life – from flesh to spirit – involved loosening himself from the synagogue, which might explain his unfortunate characterisation of synagogue-Judaism in the Galatians' allegory, but the form of the allegory makes it clear that flesh and spirit are primarily metaphors for two patterns of life: before and after conversion to Jesus Christ. It is a question of where one's loyalty lies: with sin or God, flesh or spirit. Using what has become a deracinated cliché, Paul says that we will reap what we have sown, but his actual language is about sowing in the flesh from which we reap corruption and death, and sowing in the spirit from which we reap eternal life (Galatians 6:7–10). He tells us,

> Live by the spirit ... and do not gratify the desires of the flesh. For what the flesh desires is opposed to the spirit, and what the spirit desires is opposed to the flesh; for these are opposed to each other, to prevent you from doing what you want. But if you are led by the spirit, you are not subject to the law. (5:16–18)

Then, to show that not being subject to the law does not mean lawlessness, Paul produces his sin-list of things to be avoided – fornication, idolatry, strife and the like – followed by his list of virtues: 'By contrast, the fruit of the spirit is love, joy, peace, patience, kindness, generosity, faithfulness, gentleness, and self-control' (Galatians 5: 22–23). So, beyond the rhetoric, we begin to see what might constitute a life 'in the spirit'.

Life in the spirit is possible because it is also life in the Spirit. Believers become a temple of God's Spirit (1 Corinthians 3:16) or the Holy Spirit (6:19). In Paul's language this makes each of them one of the saints, the holy ones (*hagioi*), which means they are obliged to cultivate, individually and in communities, holiness (*hagiasmos*). In the Reformed tradition, this process is usually referred to as sanctification.

Cultivating Holiness

What, then, does Paul say we have to do to become holy? It is not about feelings so much as behaviour, and not so much about pious practices as about moral behaviour. Perhaps it is because Paul thinks that holiness flourishes as a consequence of our bodies having become temples of the Holy Spirit that he emphasises the importance of bodily purity, that is, not abstinence but proper sexual behaviour.

> For this is the will of God, your sanctification: that you abstain from fornication; that each one of you knows how to control your own body in holiness and honour, not with lustful passion, like the Gentiles who do not know God; that no one wrongs or exploits a brother or sister in this matter ... For God did not call us to impurity but holiness. (1 Thessalonians 4:3–7)

We have to cleanse ourselves of defilement both in body and spirit to make holiness perfect (2 Corinthians 7:1). And in 1 Corinthians 6, Paul lists the disreputable styles of life that his converts had followed in their earlier lives – they seem to have been a particularly unappealing bunch – but he tells them they have been cleansed in baptism, made holy and righteous 'in the name of our Lord Jesus Christ and in the Spirit of our God' (6:9–11). He goes on to agree with those in Corinth who claim that they, like him, have now been released from the judgement of the law and that there is a sense in which they can say 'All things are lawful for me.' But that does not mean that all things are beneficial. Because Paul is talking about bodies and the issues that arise from our bodies being members of Christ, the example he picks here of something not being beneficial is *porneia*. This is often translated 'prostitution' but is not specifically about prostitution so much as improper sexual behaviour generally. After all Paul could hardly have thought that prostitution was ever 'lawful'.

While Paul may seem to place a disproportionate emphasis on impurity, it is not all like that. In 1 Corinthians 7 he replies to those who have asked his advice about whether to come together in marriage or, if married, whether to separate. In this chapter he suggests that a believer married to a pagan should not separate unless life has become impossible, 'for the unbelieving husband is made holy through his wife, and the unbelieving wife is made holy through her husband.' Paul thinks holiness can be catching, given a certain amount of goodwill. It is clear, then, that Paul does not think

Christians should exclude themselves from contact with pagan society to become an inward-looking (and inward-breeding) sect like the Essenes at Qumran. On the other hand, disputes between fellow believers should be settled within their own community rather than by resorting to legal action in secular courts (6:1–6). (Presumably Paul did not have to deal with reports of paedophilia, though it would not be entirely surprising if he had, given the previous history of some of those in the Corinthian church.)

Baptism makes one a fellow citizen with the saints, and cultivating holiness – the model of gardening is apt – means preparing oneself to be blameless before God (Ephesians 2:19). There is a marked eschatological emphasis on holiness: 'may he so strengthen your hearts in holiness that you may be blameless before our God and Father at the coming of our Lord Jesus with all his saints' (1 Thessalonians 3:13). There still remains a lack of content to the idea of holiness but passages from Romans push us towards 'love' and other more specific behaviours. Again Paul offers recommendations, not rules to do this and not that. The first recommendation is not to think too highly of yourself, and then to take up your role in the church in all modesty according to your gifts as teacher or prophet, or as one who shows compassion and generosity, or whatever it might be. Above all else, we must show love.

> Let love be genuine; hate what is evil, hold fast to what is good; love one another with mutual affection; outdo one another in showing honour. Do not lag in zeal, be ardent in spirit, serve the Lord. Rejoice in hope, be patient in suffering, persevere in prayer. Contribute to the needs of the saints; extend hospitality to strangers. (Romans 12:9–13)

This fullness of spirit leads us to bless those who persecute us, not curse them, which mirrors Jesus' teaching in Matthew 5.44ff and Luke 6:27ff. We must live in harmony with everyone, associate with everyone and not show snobbery. We must live peaceably with everyone and overcome evil with good (see Romans 12:14–21 at greater length and in better prose).

When it comes to the following chapter, Romans 13, Paul has often been attacked by modern critics for his gullibility about the real character of state authorities. There were certainly times when the Roman state could be vicious, as it was under Nero when Paul met his death, but it was unusually settled at the time Paul wrote Romans in the mid-50s AD. In Romans 13 Paul is being neither craven nor sycophantic: he is encouraging his readers to become good citizens. His general advice is admirable.

> Owe no one anything, except to love one another; for the one who loves another has fulfilled the law. The commandments, 'You shall not commit adultery; You shall not murder; You shall not steal; You shall not covet'; and any other commandment, are summed up in this word, 'Love your neighbour as yourself.' Love does no wrong to a neighbour; therefore, love is the fulfilling of the law. (13:8–10)

It is worth noting here that, as we shall see in the next chapter, Paul does not understand 'neighbour' to be restricted to his own social group, whether Jewish or Christian, even if that was the original sense of the commandment in Leviticus 19:18 to love one's neighbour. We should also note Paul's recommendation of generosity – God loves a cheerful giver – as the proper response to what we have received from God (2 Corinthians 9:6ff).

Finally, Paul gives an eschatological stamp to the life of holiness. Putting aside all complacency, this is how we should live, in holiness, as we wait for God to appear.

> Besides this, you know what time it is, how it is now the moment for you to wake from sleep. For salvation is nearer to us now than when we became believers; the night is far gone, the day is near. Let us then lay aside the works of darkness and put on the armour of light; let us live honourably as in the day, not in revelling and drunkenness, not in debauchery and licentiousness, not in quarrelling and jealousy. Instead put on the Lord Jesus Christ, and make no provision for the flesh, to gratify its desires. (Romans 13:11–14)

Here we see citizenship and holiness working together. Paul's idea of holiness does not draw us out of our social world. In one sense, this pattern of life is not conspicuously religious but quite ordinary. Yet at the same time it is quite extraordinary and shows what religion truly is. For Paul, it is what constitutes waiting for God – quite different from the fatuity and meaninglessness of the lives of Estragon and Vladimir as they talk their lives away while *Waiting for Godot*. Samuel Beckett's play is important for understanding modernity but, given a choice between Paul or Beckett, between meaning and hope or emptiness and despair, who makes for a better life? Paul would have echoed Zechariah's prayer that he might serve God 'without fear, in holiness and righteousness before him all our days' (Luke 1:73f).

There are two other characteristics of holiness that we have not yet mentioned: forgiveness and prayer. It seems obvious that the willingness to forgive others is part of what it is to be holy. It is what God does and God is holy. Paul, however, writes of forgiveness hardly at all. He uses the normal word for 'forgive' only in Romans 4:7 where he is quoting Psalm 32:1, and again in Colossians 1:14 where he refers to God's 'beloved son in whom we have redemption, the forgiveness of sins'. It is not clear why the theme is so infrequent in Paul. It is found in the Old Testament, though nothing like as often as one might expect, where the references are usually to having sins forgiven through the ritual of sacrificial offerings. However, as we have seen, Paul does not normally think of sin as an intentional human act but as an independent power that influences and controls us, so he does not think of sins being forgiven so much as the power of sin being *broken*. When he wants to speak of the reality of what it is to be forgiven, he uses a different language: not *aphiēmi* but *charizomai*, which is related to the word for receiving grace or kindness. Even then there are not many references and only two in what we would regard as a certainly authentic letter. He tells us that God has made us alive by forgiving our sins (Colossians 2:13), so we ought to forgive each other (Colossians 3:13; Ephesians 4:32); and once he ironically (and maybe sarcastically) asks to be forgiven when he has not actually done anything wrong (2 Corinthians 12:13). His only interesting passage on this topic relates to the fractious Corinthians.

> But if anyone has caused pain, he has caused it not to me, but to some extent – not to exaggerate it – to all of you. This

punishment by the majority is enough for such a person; so now instead you should forgive and console him, so that he may not be overwhelmed by excessive sorrow. So I urge you to reaffirm your love for him. I wrote for this reason: to test you and to know whether you are obedient in everything. Anyone whom you forgive, I also forgive. What I have forgiven, if I have forgiven anything, has been for your sake in the presence of Christ. (2 Corinthians 2:5–10)

It is clear, then, that forgiveness is a concomitant of love.

Prayer is rarely an explicit theme in Paul either, but it is mentioned in every one of his letters except Galatians, which was his sternest and most bad-tempered letter, though I am sure he did a lot of praying for the Galatians. He says enough to show that prayer is a natural constituent of the Christian life. A pattern emerges insofar as Paul usually refers to his own prayers at the beginning of his letters as part of his formal introductions, while his references to the prayers of his readers tend to be at the end. This suggests that the greetings which start his letters are more than pious formalities, they are genuine prayers of a sort: 'grace to you and peace from God our Father and the Lord Jesus Christ' (1 Corinthians 1:3). More than once he asks his readers to pray for him (1 Thessalonians 5:25; 2 Thessalonians 3:1; Ephesians 6:18). They should pray without ceasing (1 Thessalonians 5:17) and 'devote themselves to prayer, keeping alert with thanksgiving' (Colossians 4:2). And how should they pray? Mainly with thanksgiving, that all may be worthy of their call, that Christ might be glorified in them, that their love might overflow with knowledge and insight to help them determine what is best (Philippians 1:9), and for the success of the work of Paul and his companions. Romans 15:13 is one of not many examples of one of his prayers: 'May the God of hope fill you with all joy and peace in believing, so that you may abound in hope by the power of the Holy Spirit.'

Paul would certainly have known the Lord's Prayer in some form (Matthew 6:9–13; Luke 11:2–4) as is confirmed when he says that we address God as Abba, Father (Romans 8:15). He tells us not to worry but to let our requests be made known to God in prayer

(Philippians 4:6). Yet his most encouraging advice is for those who find prayer difficult:

> The Spirit helps us in our weakness; for we do not know how to pray as we ought, but that very Spirit intercedes with sighs too deep for words. And God, who searches the heart, knows what is the mind of the Spirit, because the Spirit intercedes for the saints according to the will of God. (Romans 8:26–27)

Perhaps holiness is not so very difficult or remarkable after all, once the power of sin has been broken, once one has become one of the saints, through baptism into membership of the church.

9

Unity

Factions

Looking back on my days as an undergraduate, I recall a number of
my teachers and fellow students being directly involved in the
formation of the United Reformed Church, which came about by
bringing together two churches in England and Wales from the
Reformed, i.e. Calvinist, tradition: the Congregational Church and
the small Presbyterian Church. There was a mood of celebration
when this was achieved in 1972, but there were a few diehard
Congregationalists and Presbyterians who had principled objections to the terms on which unity had been achieved and they
remained outside the new church. The outcome of this push for
unity was that there were now three churches instead of two: a large
group of United Reformers and two smaller denominations. (A few
years later in 1981 the Disciples of Christ, including some Scottish
congregations, joined the URC.) This proliferation of denominations has been a characteristic of the Protestant tradition since the
Reformation, mitigated by a desire during the past one hundred
years in the Ecumenical Movement to unify churches but sometimes resulting in the emergence of large churches with smaller
satellites, as with the example of the URC. While this multiple
fragmentation is characteristic of Protestantism, other traditions are
not immune from comparable tendencies. The Orthodox and
Anglican Communion divide into national churches, which can
occasionally devolve into rank nationalism, as when the Serbian
Orthodox Church supported the Milošević government during the
break-up of Yugoslavia in the 1990s. Roman Catholics put a higher
value on unity and ecclesiastical conformity but even here factions

break away like the Tridentinist Society of St Pius X (which has a history of anti-Semitism and sympathy for fascism). It goes without saying that unity is something to be valued but, on the other hand, the preservation of unity at all costs can encourage authoritarian leadership and the suppression of dissent – in outward appearance at least, because in practice churches have limited power to deal with dissent and enforce uniformity. As Stalin said in a different context, they do not have enough tanks.

Fragmentation and factionalism among churches represent a failure of the Pauline patrimony. If there was one thing Paul struggled to achieve throughout his Christian life, it was unity within his local churches and in the church at large. This comes out most clearly in that most practical of his letters, 1 Corinthians. Right in the opening chapter, he notes the reports he has received from 'Chloe's people' about their quarrelling. They had formed in-groups in Corinth that identified themselves with different leaders, none of whom were from Corinth: Paul, Apollos, Cephas/Peter and Christ. On the basis of those names it is impossible to know what they were quarrelling about. Did they perhaps enjoy arguing for its own sake?

It might have been the case that all the educated inhabitants of that most cosmopolitan of cities wanted to identify with one of the many philosophers and religious teachers who passed through Corinth. The city seems to have been a hotbed of New Age religions and philosophies from which a citizen could take his pick. Could it have been that the Christians, poorly educated as they seem to have been (1 Corinthians 1:26), sought to achieve some cultural status by patronising a religious teacher of their own? That might have been why Apollos was more highly regarded than Paul, whose speech was 'not with plausible words of wisdom' (2:4). If that were the case, the Christians at Corinth were still attached to social expectations which had nothing to do with the gospel. Paul was not interested in his status as a teacher or his reputation as a smooth talker, i.e., one skilled in rhetoric. He makes it clear that his task above all else was to proclaim a crucified Christ/Messiah, which for sophisticated Greeks was a foolish idea and for pious Jews was self-contradictory and a stumbling-block (1:21–25). His responsibility was to bring the believers in Corinth to the power of the cross of Christ, for, while the cross as a worldly symbol is a sign of powerlessness and weakness, 'Christ is the power of God ... and God's weakness is stronger than human strength' (1:24f).

What, then, was the true status of Paul and Apollos in Corinth? Paul planted the community, Apollos (of whom Paul speaks only good things) watered it, but it was God who gave it growth. They were God's servants, working together on the Corinthians who were 'God's field, God's building' (3:9). The foundation was and remains Jesus Christ (3:11). Everything the Corinthians have has been *received* as a gift, as grace, so they have no reason to boast, for what they have is not a result of their own efforts (4:7). In the early chapters of this letter we see the first indications of a problem that Paul had to deal with more explicitly later: elitism. The Corinthians formed their social attachments as a way of asserting their own superiority, albeit a spiritual superiority, which had the effect of denigrating fellow Christians who were aligned to other factions. This had a particularly unfortunate effect on their communal worship and their celebration of the Eucharist.

The ritual meal that is the re-enactment of the Last Supper was celebrated in Corinth, and presumably in other local churches at that time, as a full meal. The problem in Corinth was that

> when you come together as a church [i.e. an assembly, an *ekklēsia*], I hear that there are divisions among you ... For when the time comes to eat, each of you goes ahead with your own supper, and one goes hungry and another becomes drunk. What! Do you not have homes to eat and drink in? Or do you show contempt for the church of God and humiliate those who have nothing? (1 Corinthians 11:18, 21–22)

Paul's recommendation was that when they come together, they should wait for each other, and if anyone needs feeding, they should do it at home (11:33f). It may be that the architectural style of the house they met in exacerbated the problem. Jerome Murphy-O'Connor thinks that the Christian community, which would have numbered a few dozen, could not have been seated in any one room for a meal. On the basis of the excavation of one house in Corinth and the assumption that this was a typical house, Murphy-

O'Connor has suggested that the host would have presided in the main room with his close friends, whom he would have invited to arrive early (for drinks?), while the rest would have been accommodated outside the door in a long corridor, separate from the main group but within hearing distance.[1] Whether or not this was the case, the problem remains the same: the elitism of a self-appointed group to the exclusion and even humiliation of the rest. This is clearly not what Paul wanted.

Jews and Gentiles

The division that concerned Paul most was the one between Jews and Gentiles. Paul came from a strict Pharisaic background, albeit from a Hellenised tradition that used the Greek version of the Jewish scriptures. He describes himself as having been zealous in observance of the law and, for reasons of keeping purity and preserving holiness according to the Torah, he would have had no more contact with non-Jews than was strictly necessary. We have already seen that holiness in the Old Testament involves separation, which leads to a religion of binary opposites. In such a religion the world becomes divided into the sacred and the secular, the clean and unclean, the holy and profane; a world in which God is separated from the people, and the holy people is separated from the sinful nations. The priests – only men and only from the tribe of Levi – are mediators who represent the people before the holy God and, while on priestly duty, are separated from lay people, especially women. Only the High Priest can enter the Holy of Holies to be in the presence of God and then only once a year on the Day of Atonement. To take part in formal worship any Jew must be in a state of ritual purity. Some foods are acceptable and others not. It is a religion of distinctions; distinctions of race, of gender, of social class and states of being, both ritual and moral. And the God-given mark of Jewish identity is above all circumcision (Genesis 17:9–14).

Paul was steeped in this Jewish world, circumcised on the eighth day and blameless in his observance of the law of Moses (Philippians

---

1 J. Murphy-O'Connor, *Keys to First Corinthians: Revisiting the Major Issues* (Oxford: OUP, 2009), ch. 12, 'House Churches and the Eucharist', pp. 182–93.

3:5f). What turned him against all this? It was not in the first place a result of argument but of experience. Whatever exactly happened to him on the Damascus road – there are three slightly different accounts of the event in Acts but no description from Paul himself – he understood it to be a vision of the risen Christ, comparable with the sightings that the other apostles had had. Every conviction of Paul's later life is rooted in that experience. Although he did not put it this way, that event showed him that God had done something new in history and that Moses is no longer enough. Paul never lost his conviction that the Torah is a divine gift and to that extent it cannot be overturned (Romans 9:4; 11:29), but he thought it had lost its effectiveness in these new circumstances. If the law, given through Moses, had been enough for salvation, there would have been no need for the Christ-event. As Paul puts it, 'if righteousness comes through the law, then Christ died for nothing' (Galatians 2:21). Yet there has been a Christ-event, in which a man condemned by Roman and Jewish law has, Paul is firmly convinced, been raised from the dead by God. He believes that God has done something which transcends the Torah, something which has led us into a new period in human history in which the Torah is not abrogated, but pushed into the background. It is no longer, as a whole, relevant to the new age and is no longer the measure by which Paul would live his life. The law is dead, it is no longer life-giving. The law has reached its goal (*telos*, both perfection and termination) in Christ (Romans 10:4).

The problem with the Torah was that the Jews had it and the Gentiles didn't. The law had been a barrier to Gentiles who had been prevented from entering into a covenant with God and achieving righteousness. Indeed the Torah's ritual requirements were very effective in keeping Gentiles out of the covenant and in effect it turned Judaism into a national and tribal religion. In preserving the distinction between the holy and the profane, embedded in particular rituals, the law effectively excluded the

Gentiles.[2] The Torah could do great things in its time but it had its limitations. With the death and resurrection of Christ, Paul came to see that righteousness, or salvation, or 'deliverance' as Douglas Campbell calls it,[3] no longer comes from a life lived according to Torah, but from *pistis*: belief, trust in and faithfulness to Christ as the representative, indeed the incarnation, of God.

We have seen that there has been a marked shift in recent years in the traditional understanding of what Paul means by justification by faith, though no consensus has yet been achieved. Whether one shares the new perspective on Paul or sticks to a more traditional Lutheran reading, one thing that all agree on is that 'justification' theology means that salvation is available for the whole human race without distinction, and one of the things that Paul was trying to do was lay a theological foundation for including Gentiles alongside Jews in God's covenant.

Circumcision, the Symbol of Salvation?

As the Apostle to the Gentiles, Paul had to fight a rearguard action against those Christian Pharisees, known as Judaisers. They would only accept Gentiles into the church if they took on the full obligations of Torah, so that in effect they ceased to be Gentiles and the church would become no more than a messianic version of the synagogue. He also had to hold back those Gentile converts who were being lured by the Judaisers into taking on the obligations of the Torah as necessary parts of the Christian life.

To get the logical force of Paul's argument it is necessary to bounce back and forth between Galatians and Romans. Paul dic-

---

2 This is only relatively true because the Talmud holds that Gentiles can become righteous and have a place in the world to come by keeping the Noahide covenant, though Paul does not discuss this because the Talmud was published long after his time. The Noahide Code comprises seven laws given to Noah in Genesis: the prohibitions against idolatry; murder; theft; sexual immorality (adultery, incest, bestiality); and blasphemy; the dietary law not to eat flesh taken from an animal while it was still alive; and the requirement to have a just legal system.

3 Douglas A. Campbell, *The Deliverance of God: An Apocalyptic Reading of Justification in Paul* (Grand Rapids, MI: Eerdmans, 2009).

tated his letters to a secretary, which meant that he sometimes missed out steps in his argument and the reader has to fill the gaps by extracting bits from other letters. Paul's first step in his argument with the Gentile believers in Galatia, who sought circumcision, is to tell them that if they seek salvation through an act commanded in the Torah, they are in effect reverting to an earlier stage of human history, the age before Christ, and, to succeed down that route, they must take on *all* the obligations that are spelt out in the Torah (Galatians 5:2–3). It is not just a question of circumcision, but *everything*. The second step of the argument is to claim that no one has succeeded in keeping all the Torah's commandments because Jews are as much under the power of sin as are Gentiles (Romans 3:9). To justify this he produces a catena of scriptural quotations, from Psalms and Isaiah (Romans 3:10–18 citing Psalms 14:1–2; 53:1–2; 5:9; 140:3; 10:7 and Isaiah 59:7–8 from the Greek Bible where the Psalm numbers are slightly different). The third step is to quote Deuteronomy to show that a curse is placed on anyone who does not succeed in keeping *all* the commandments: 'Cursed is everyone who does not observe and obey all the things written in the book of the law' (Deuteronomy 27:26 quoted at Galatians 3:10). The implication of step two is that every Jew is under the curse of Deuteronomy, because they have taken upon themselves the obligation of observing the Torah and, Paul alleges, have not succeeded in fulfilling it all. This part of the argument relies on scriptural proof rather than observation of anyone's actual behaviour.

What exactly is this curse? We must assume it to be death, for it is sin that causes people's failure to keep the law fully (Romans 3:9) and, since the time of the first couple in Genesis, the punishment for sin has been death. God made Adam and his descendants subject to mortality for having disobeyed his one command: not to eat the fruit of the tree of the knowledge of good and evil (Genesis 3). So the law promises life but does not have the power to deliver it. Accepting circumcision takes a man down a pathway that is destined to fail. Something else is required for salvation and, Paul believes, that something is Jesus Christ. What Christ did resulted in God raising him from the dead, overcoming the inevitability of death and showing that the power of sin has been broken at last.

The final step in the argument concerns the obligation laid on Abraham in Genesis 17 to circumcise all his male descendants on the eighth day after their birth. Paul deals with this in Galatians 3 and Romans 4. Abraham was counted a righteous man because he believed God's promises that he would become the father of a great nation and that God would give them a land to live in (Romans 4:3 quoting Genesis 15:6). In the Genesis narrative, Abraham acquired his righteous status in chapter 15, *before* he had been instructed in chapter 17 to circumcise, showing that righteousness comes from grace, not any human action in fulfilment of a law. Abraham, then, had no reason to boast of any achievement and, by implication, nor does Paul, nor the Corinthians, nor anyone else. God's having given the law at a later time does not change this state of affairs:

> the law, which came four hundred and thirty years later, does not annul a covenant previously ratified by God, so as to nullify the promise. For if the inheritance comes from the law, it no longer comes from the promise; but God granted it to Abraham through the promise. (Galatians 3:17f)

Paul's argument not only shows why circumcision has never been a ritual requirement of Christian practice but it also has the unexpected outcome of claiming that followers of Jesus not only have Abraham as their spiritual father but that they alone are his true descendants. It is the children of the promise who constitute the true Israel, which is spelt out in more detail in the allegory of the two covenants of Galatians 4:21–31. In Galatians, moreover, Paul goes one important stage further. In Genesis 17 Abraham is commanded to circumcise himself and his descendants as a sign of the covenant God has established with him. For a Jew, circumcision is the sign of the covenant and, while its value has been questioned in some liberal Jewish discussions on grounds of health or the undesirability of unnecessary surgery, this is irrelevant for understanding what it is about in Genesis. Jews are circumcised because God commanded it. Paul's problem is that it is a sign which is restricted to men and to Jewish men (the later emergence of Islam is irrelevant for understanding Paul on this issue). From reading Paul you might think the practice was restricted to *free* Jewish men, but in the Old

Testament period male slaves were also circumcised. Nonetheless, as a sign of the covenant, circumcision has its limitations. In Christianity, the sign of the new covenant in Jesus Christ is baptism, which is available to *all* who believe it, so for Paul, baptism is a more inclusive sign of a more inclusive covenant. Baptism can be received by *anyone* without distinction of race, social status or gender:

> in Christ Jesus you are all children of God through faith. As many of you as were baptized into Christ have clothed yourselves with Christ. There is no longer Jew or Greek, there is no longer slave or free, there is no longer male or female; for all of you are one in Christ Jesus. (Galatians 3:26–28).

Obviously as a fact of life there still are men and women, still different races and still social classes. Paul has not given us a charter for political equality here. It is important to read this passage in its context in the letter to Galatia where one can see that the discussion is about baptism, and baptism as a sign of inclusion into a covenant which is for everyone, with Jesus as the mediator of that covenant (see Hebrews 8:6; 9:15).

Paul was also able to revive an older Jewish idea that true circumcision is spiritual, a matter of the 'heart', not something just external and physical (Romans 2:28f, referring to, but not quoting, Deuteronomy 10:16; 30:6; Jeremiah 4:4; 9:20f). This means that God now shows no partiality between Jew and Gentile (Romans 2:11), which leads Paul to the great line that sums up the Christian life: 'in Christ Jesus neither circumcision nor uncircumcision counts for anything; the only thing that counts is faith working through love' (Galatians 5:6).

Men and Women

Paul does not have a great deal to say about distinctions of social class. What little he does say is mainly about slaves and slave-masters and we have already seen how Paul gives a new sense to what we might mean by slavery when he speaks of becoming a slave of Christ. If he did not see the full social implications of this, he can hardly be singled out from the other men of his age for blame. From our standpoint, we might have hoped for more from what he said about women. On the one hand, what he says about the status of women, particularly in regard to marriage, is remarkable for a Jewish man in the first century (1 Corinthians 7 – it is by no means clear that he is the author of the domestic advice in Colossians 3:18–19 and Ephesians 5:21–33), but elsewhere, in other contexts, concerning public worship for example, he failed to escape the cultural limitations of his time. Women have to remain subordinate, he says, and must not speak in assemblies. If they want to know anything, they must ask their husband at home (1 Corinthians 14:34f). When praying or prophesying, women have to cover their heads (11:2–16), though it is now hard to know why this should have been an important issue. Paul struggles to balance the social subordination of women (11:8–9) with the mutual interdependence of men and women (11:11–12) and in the end his bizarre argument on head-covering crumbles into an authoritarian assertion that 'we have no such custom, nor do the churches of God' (11:16), as though he realised his argument was unconvincing.

The Weak and the Strong

Paul's concern with elitism can also be seen in his solicitude for those whose faith might be fragile. These were recent converts who had not yet fully absorbed the implications of Christian freedom. The immediate issue was about food and what might legitimately be eaten. The social context in Corinth was that of paganism rather than Judaism, and the problem was that in almost any city of the Empire the meat on sale at market stalls might well have been sacrificed to pagan gods. Did cooking and eating this meat involve one in idolatry? The response of some of those first Christians, because of their scruples about having anything to do with pagan-ism, was to become vegetarian (Romans 14:2). Paul regards these apparently very religious people as weak in faith because their allegiance to Christ could be easily damaged by seeing others behaving in a more relaxed way, eating meat without scruple and even eating in pagan temples. The strong in faith firmly believed that 'God is one' and idols are nothing, so anything can be eaten. It is not something worth worrying about. The situation reminds me of the occasion when I visited a Hindu temple with a colleague and a group of students. We removed our shoes, covered our heads and sat down for a short talk. We were then offered fruit and nuts which had been taken from a basket in front of the statue of a Hindu god. Because of his beliefs, one of the group had reservations about eating an offering to 'an idol'. I suggested he eat it because it was just a gesture of hospitality, and I think that was the more authentically Pauline response. Paul thinks an invited guest should be prepared to eat anything – unless there is deliberate provocation. Paul thinks the division between the sacred and the profane has been abolished and nothing is unclean in itself (14:14) – that clearly covers the food regulations of Judaism. While the church has encouraged spiritual practices of abstaining from certain foods at certain times, Christianity has never had any necessary rules about what one might eat. The only thing that might be 'lawful but not beneficial' is greed.

What concerns us here is how Paul guides those who think they are free to eat anything anywhere, so that they do nothing to disturb those whose faith, in his terms, is weak, those who might be offended by what they see as compromises with paganism. Paul did not want any ritual practice or social custom to get in the way of the reception of the gospel.

> For though I am free with respect to all, I have made myself a slave to all, so that I might win more of them. To the Jews I became as a Jew, in order to win Jews. To those under the law I became as one under the law ... so that I might win those under the law. To those outside the law I became as one outside the law ... so that I might win those outside the law. To the weak I became weak, so that I might win the weak. I have become all things to all people, so that I might by any means save some. I do it all for the sake of the gospel. (1 Corinthians 9:19–23)

To the weak he became like one who is weak. To hold everyone together in a unified church, Paul urges the strong not to provoke those who might be scandalised by their eating in temples or eating what may be regarded as unclean food. It is one thing to have knowledge of what constitutes the freedom of the gospel but it is another to have love for one's fellow believer by not damaging their conscience (1 Corinthians 8:7–13; Romans 14). Paul always looks for peace and mutual upbuilding.

The Body of Christ

The mutuality of fellow believers finds expression in Paul's image of the church as the body of Christ, though he uses the idea in only two places in his definitely authentic letters: 1 Corinthians 12:12–27 and Romans 12:4ff – as well as in Colossians and Ephesians. (I am passing over the references to 'body' in 1 Corinthians 11 which are clearly eucharistic, and also in 1 Corinthians 10 which are primarily eucharistic, though the author slips almost unobtrusively from the eucharistic meaning to the ecclesial meaning in v. 17.) It is a simple idea: believers are each members of the same living organism with Christ its head, where *kephalē* can mean 'head' both literally and metaphorically (i.e., chief person) and can also mean 'origin'. In this body, we are told to avoid elitism, for God has arranged it that socially inferior members receive the greater honour. Mutuality means that if one suffers, all suffer; and if one is honoured, all share the joy. Ephesians is the letter that uses the image of body more than any other as a way of emphasising unity, referring to God having created 'one new humanity in place of the two', meaning that the old division between Jew and Gentile has been removed (Ephesians 2:11–22).

The metaphor of 'the body of Christ' provides the context for Paul dealing with the spiritual gifts, or charisms (*charismata*, from the word for grace or favour), that one might receive in the church. He presents a hierarchy of these in 1 Corinthians 12: apostleship, prophecy, teaching, performing acts of power (miracles) or gifts of healing, forms of assistance or leadership, and speaking in tongues. In one respect these charisms had become a problem in Corinth. Paul first makes it clear that no one person is going to have all these charisms. Perhaps some thought that they did not have any of these gifts, though the list is so broad – Romans adds ministering, exhorting, giving generously, being compassionate and cheerful (12:7f) – that everyone ought to be able to offer something for the good of the community. The problem was with speaking in tongues.

Paul did not disapprove of 'tongues' because he did it himself and he wished that others could do it too (how far did he really think that?). For those who are not familiar with it, speaking or singing in tongues is normally a way of praising God either by using sounds or nonsense words or stereotyped expressions of praise. One might call it 'holy chuntering'. It is not informative. For information you need a prophet who can interpret what the tongues might mean. At its worst, speaking in tongues can be a form of self-indulgence and Paul hints at its limitation when he says that those who speak in tongues build up themselves, while those who prophesy build up the church (1 Corinthians 14:2–5). Speaking in tongues can be a spectacular activity, but in chapter 14 Paul seeks to put it in its place. He says he would rather speak five meaningful words of instruction than ten thousand words in a tongue. The problem in Corinth seems to have been that the speakers-in-tongues were getting above themselves and seeing their gift as a sign of their spiritual superiority. Paul's line is that prophecy and the interpretation of tongues are superior because they are intelligible. Also, because they are gifts of the Spirit, no one has anything to boast about. Not everyone can have all of these gifts, but everyone can have something that builds up the community. And there is a yet more excellent way that everyone can share: love, *agapē*. Paul's celebrated eulogy to love comes right in the middle of his discussion of charisms – 1 Corinthians 13 is bracketed by chapters 12 and 14 on spiritual gifts. Whatever charism one may or may not have, everyone must show love. Elitism, division and quarrelling have no place in the body of Christ. Of course, human weakness and sin being what they are means there will always be problems and certainly apostolic Christianity does not represent a golden age of exemplary behaviour. Nonetheless, Christians in the modern church can still learn a lot from Paul's quest for unity. Squabbles about one's own aesthetic preferences in worship, for example, do not work for the healthy building up of the church, nor does the imposition of officious decisions. One can hardly overestimate the importance of unity in the Christian life but it is not something that the church has been conspicuously successful at.

10

Life in Christ

The Christian life is a life lived in Christ. Thus far our account of
Paul has focused on his understanding of the practice of Christian
life and the virtues that underpin it. We have been moving in an area
where ethics and spirituality overlap, supported by an understanding
of Paul's theology. But at the end, his theology has to take centre
stage because Paul does not see the Christian life as just an ethical
choice, one among many, as one might, in Paul's time, have chosen
to be a Stoic or a Cynic or an Epicurean. The Christian life may have
its appeal as a practice of life (let us not say 'lifestyle') for those who
see themselves in a society where so many people seem to live
superficial and sometimes even chaotic and dissolute lives – though
a life that opts for humility and low status is not likely to appeal to
everyone. In the end, however, the Christian life cannot be
detached from Jesus Christ himself and this chapter is likely to take
on a more confessional tone as we look at the foundation of Paul's
vision. Paul the Jew adopted the Christian life (though he would
not have called it that) because of what he came to believe about
Jesus, a belief rooted in what he had experienced of Jesus as the now
risen Christ, on that Damascus road, supported by what he had
been told by the original eye-witnesses. We must then turn to Paul's
theology and specifically to his Christology to understand what was
the driving force behind his new life.

In Christ

'In Christ' is an expression that Paul uses 58 times (and 16 more
times in Colossians and Ephesians). This is a distinctly Pauline phrase
that is used hardly anywhere else in the New Testament and never in

the Gospels. He has variations on it: 'with Christ' occurs 4 times (plus 4 in Colossians and Ephesians) and 'in the Lord' 35 times (plus 12 in Colossians and Ephesians). The phrases go together, amounting to 97 occurrences in the authentic letters, for, as we shall see, Christ (*Christos*) and Lord (*kurios*) are two distinctive titles that Paul gives to Jesus. This phrase-group can be found in all Paul's letters and is more pervasive than 'justification by faith', which is largely concentrated in just two letters. This is clearly a major theme in Paul and has led a number of writers to suggest that it is better to see 'in Christ' as the central point of Paul's theology rather than 'justification', which has held that privileged position at least since the time of Luther. As traditionally understood, justification has been about how individuals, despite their faults, can stand uncondemned before God, and the answer is: by faith not works. Salvation comes from God as grace, free gift, not from human effort. Rather differently, 'in Christ' is said to point to the believer having a shared life with Christ; living, in some sense, *in* Christ. The key words that have been introduced into the debate to indicate the implications of living in Christ are 'participation' and 'transformation' – having one's life transformed through participating in the life of the risen Christ. When combined with the idea of being a member of the body of Christ, i.e., the church, this has a less individualistic sense than justification by faith has been given. However, some writers in the past have tended to over-interpret the idea of life 'in Christ' by using it as a lever for speaking about Paul's 'mysticism'. Albert Schweitzer, in stressing union with Christ, even went so far as to make the silly comment that the believer has a *physical* relation with Christ, which can only have resulted from Schweitzer's failure to see that being a part of the body of Christ is a metaphor.[1]

So what did Paul mean by being 'in Christ' and those other similar expressions? There is no single answer to this. Many of the uses, around a third, are simply to do with *identity* and are the

---

1   A. Schweitzer, *The Mysticism of Paul the Apostle* (London: Black, 1931), p. 127. The full quotation is, 'That what is in view in the Pauline mysticism is an actual physical union between Christ and the elect is proved by the fact that "being in Christ" corresponds to and, as a state of existence, takes the place of the physical "being in the flesh".'

equivalent of identifying someone as Christian. It is significant that the word 'Christian' only occurs three times in the New Testament and never in Paul (Acts 11:26; 26:28; 1 Peter 4.16). In the middle of the first century there was no independent religion to be identified as Christianity and in the absence of that label, 'in Christ' was Paul's way of identifying a fellow believer (see, for example, Romans 8:1; 1 Corinthians 1:2; Philippians 1:1; 4:21). To refer to the Christian church or Christianity in Paul's time, as I have sometimes done, is just a convenience. There is no strong theological content to this usage of 'in Christ'.

A second common use, perhaps another third of the cases, points to *the practice of the Christian life*. These often overlap with the first group but have a stronger content because they suggest that 'in Christ' is not just a badge of identity but points to something of the content of what it is to be Christian, where the content is about practice rather than belief. So in his earliest letter, Paul tells the Thessalonians to be imitators of the churches 'in Christ' in Judea because they have suffered from the Gentiles in the same way as the Judean Christians have suffered from their Jewish neighbours (1 Thessalonians 2:14). Here being in Christ means imitating others in how they deal with persecution. In the next letter, 2 Thessalonians, being in Christ means working quietly and earning your living so as not to sponge off others. Because they keep quarrelling and creating factions, Paul regards the Corinthians as babies in Christ, not yet ready for solid food (1 Corinthians 3:1), though when he calls Timothy his 'beloved and faithful child in the Lord', he indicates something very positive about Timothy's character, for it is he who will remind those in Corinth 'of my ways in Christ Jesus' (1 Corinthians 4:17). Other uses point to the wisdom (1 Corinthians 4:10), love (16:24), liberty (Galatians 2:4) and triumph of the Christian life (2 Corinthians 2:14). In Romans 9:1 being in Christ involves speaking the truth. Philippians was written from prison and in that letter Paul refers to his imprisonment (literally 'chains') being 'in Christ' (1:13) and he contrasts this with the encouragement (2:1) and peace (4:7) that comes from having 'the same mind ... that was in Christ Jesus' (2:5). Paul tells his readers in Philippi to live their lives in a manner worthy of the gospel of Christ (1:27). So saying someone is in Christ is not just a means of identifying a person as

145

part of a particular social group but can also indicate something of the pattern of life that follows from being in that social group. Every action has to be performed 'in Christ' and then one can experience joy 'in the Lord' (Philippians 2:29). In these passages there are moral and spiritual allusions that point to an individual becoming Christ-like, but still nothing that would suggest a mystical union with Christ.

A third category is about divine *agency* – what God has done 'in Christ' – and provides important material for Paul's Christology. This deals with how God has chosen to act on the human race: in Christ. This is how the invisible, unknowable God of the Old Testament presents himself: in the face of Christ (2 Corinthians 4:6). Paul's idea is that God has a plan, a long-term plan, but for this to be known God has to use human agents: Abraham, Moses, the kings – some of them – and the prophets. Without these agents we would know nothing of what God is up to. In these latter days, God has acted through Jesus (see also Hebrews 1:1–2). Ephesians is clearest about this where Paul (if it is he) says he has received grace to bring the gospel to the Gentiles,

> and to make everyone see what is the plan of the mystery hidden for ages in God ... so that through the church the wisdom of God ... might now be made known ... This was in accordance with the eternal purpose that he has carried out in Christ Jesus our Lord. (Ephesians 3:9–11)

What has happened in Christ is that God's plan to include Gentiles in salvation has been revealed, so making it possible for the human race to become unified and for all people to be reconciled with God. As this means that Jews and Gentiles are to be saved on the same basis, the plan must ease the law into the background because the Gentiles do not have the law and are not going to be saved by it. All can be made righteous by God's grace, 'through the redemption that is in Christ Jesus' (Romans 3:24) not through the law. It is in Christ that God's blessing on Abraham has finally come to the Gentiles, a blessing that Paul associates with the Spirit, so that they may now live 'in the Spirit' (Galatians 3:14). In a general way of speaking, Paul tells his readers that it is in Christ that they have received God's love (Romans 8:39), his grace (1 Corinthians 1:4), his blessings (Ephesians 1:3), and in whom God supplies their every need (Philippians 4:19), where all four expressions mean much the same thing. It is in Christ that we have become dead to sin and alive to God (Romans 6:11; 8:2), and this life is eternal life, 'for the wages of sin is death, but the free gift of God is eternal life in Christ Jesus our Lord' (6:23). Here 'eternal' does not just mean unending but of a different order. We have received reconciliation ('God was in Christ reconciling the world to himself', 2 Corinthians 5:19), have been counted righteous ('justified in Christ', Galatians 2:17) and become children of God (3:26). It is God's will in Christ that you give thanks in everything (1 Thessalonians 5:18) and Paul boasts of what God has done in Christ (Romans 15:17). It is in Christ that God has removed the veil that has masked the understanding of the Jews when they read the law (2 Corinthians 3:14).

This is a sizeable number of references that show that God acts 'in Christ' as his agent in the world. They clearly give Jesus a high status; they portray him as a mediator, as a priest would be in Old Testament religion, though one of many and not unique. However, there is yet a fourth category, a smaller group, linked with our second category where 'in Christ' points to acting in a Christlike way, but this group takes the matter further. These are the passages that point to having a *shared life with Christ*, where one may participate in some real (but not physical) way in the life of the risen Christ. This sense of being in Christ is reinforced on three occasions where Paul reverses the order and speaks of Christ dwelling in a person. Paul asks if you realise that Jesus Christ is in you (2 Corinthians 13:5) and also says,

> Anyone who does not have the Spirit of Christ does not belong to him. But if Christ is in you, though the body is dead because of sin, the Spirit is life because of righteousness. (Romans 8:9f)

In two other places he speaks of clothing yourself with Christ (Galatians 3:37; Romans 13:14) and Colossians and Ephesians refer to putting on a new self. But, by this stage of development, putting on a new self and putting on Christ amount to much the same thing (Colossians 3:9–10; Ephesians 4:22–24).

Yet is 'participation' the right word to describe the believer's relation to Christ? At best there are only hints of a quasi-participation in these passages and we must be cautious about claiming too much on their basis. The key line in this discussion is Galatians 2:19–20: 'I have been crucified with Christ; and it is no longer I who live, but it is Christ who lives in me.' Here there is indeed a suggestion of Paul losing his identity in Christ. The line is related to life and death, dying either metaphorically or literally and rising to life. So in Adam all are subject to death but now all will be made alive in Christ (1 Corinthians 15:22). The Thessalonians are told that those who have already died in Christ will rise first at the final resurrection, then those who are still alive will be taken up and will be 'with the Lord' for ever (1 Thessalonians 4:16–18). Indeed it is the 'with Christ' and 'with the Lord' passages that press the participation case most strongly. Yet to say someone has died in Christ normally refers to baptism and does little more than identify them as Christian, and to be with the Lord at the resurrection, in Philippians 1:23f, is about location rather than participation, as in 'I am hard pressed between the two: my desire is to depart and be with Christ, for that is far better; but to remain in the flesh is more necessary for you.'

In the following chapter, 'Let the same mind be in you that was in Christ Jesus' (Philippians 2:5) means to think in the same way as Christ, to see the world in the same way and to follow the same pattern of life as Christ. Paul tells us in Galatians that 'in Christ' circumcision or its absence counts for nothing (5:6), nor does whether you are Jew or Greek, male or female, slave or free (3:28). Everyone shares a spiritual solidarity by being 'one body in Christ' (Romans 12:5). Ephesians uses an architectural model to develop this idea, in which members of the church are said to be citizens of the household of God, which has apostles and prophets as its foundation and Jesus as its cornerstone, so the body of Christ is now called 'a holy temple in the Lord' (Ephesians 2:19–22).

One reason for Paul using 'in Christ' language is as a contrast with 'in Adam', to make it clear that a historical and spiritual change has taken place in humanity and that Paul and his readers live in a new era. For those who live 'in Christ' all things have been renewed, there is a new creation (2 Corinthians 5:17). If you have died in baptism, you have to seek the things which are above, where Christ is, for 'your life is hidden with Christ in God' (Colossians 3:1–3). There are hints of something unique here – Christ is certainly far more than a moral example to be emulated – but the idea of participation in the life of Christ is not strongly supported. It could be argued that one participates in the church and so in the body of Christ but that does not seem to be the sense of Paul's language. Paul certainly believes in moral and spiritual transformation but that in itself does not point to Paul being a mystic. Let us try to approach him from a different direction.

Spiritual Identification in Christ

There have been tendencies in the history of Christian piety to exalt Jesus far above the rest of humanity. This first began at the end of the first century when the Christian Gnostics went so far as to deny that Jesus was human at all: he was God but not God incarnate. Gnosticism seems to have been originally an independent religion that predated Christianity. Its main characteristic is a dualism which divides the world into two realms, the spiritual and the material, in which matter is bad and spirit is good. Jesus Christ was seen by the Gnostics to be the divine saviour who would release his followers from the material world to enjoy a purely spiritual life with God. (To complicate matters the Christian Gnostics believed in two Gods: the Old Testament God who created the material world and a superior God who would not dirty his hands with that sort of thing.) As Saviour, then, Jesus could have nothing physical about him. His bodily existence was an illusion, for our benefit but with no substance to it. He was divine but not in any real sense human. The formulation of the doctrine of the incarnation from the Fourth Gospel onwards was an attempt, not to explain, but to assert that Jesus was (and is) divine *and* human. This doctrine means that in one sense Jesus is to be identified with God, and in another sense he is to be identified with us. In the course of Christian history, his followers have often found it hard to keep a balance and have tended to lean one way or the other, giving undue emphasis to his divinity or to his humanity. With the development of the doctrine of the Trinity, developed historically in parallel with the doctrine of the incarnation, Jesus was defined as the Son of God the Father, the second person of the Trinity and co-equal with the Father and the Spirit. Jesus quickly became the object of worship, the one to whom prayer is addressed, the one exalted into the heavens. The Gnostics would have approved all this but they went further to deny any humanity to Jesus. But you do not have to be a full-blown Gnostic to fail to fully appreciate – subconsciously perhaps – Jesus' humanity when acknowledging his place in the Godhead. There are many Christians who would claim to be perfectly orthodox but fail to do his humanity justice. The Christology of the Gnostics is known as Docetism (from *dokein*, to seem, as in 'Jesus seemed to be human but wasn't really') but there can also be a semi-docetism that leans in the same direction without actually denying that Jesus was one of us, a member of the human race. Here the assertion that Jesus was human is fragile and carries insufficient weight. This tendency to semi-docetism has the effect of opening up a gap between Jesus and the rest of us. There is no such tendency in Paul.

Paul repeatedly asserts that those who follow Jesus, those who are faithful to him, share the pattern of his life and his destiny. Along with Christ and Lord, Paul gives the title Son to Jesus as he affirms that Jesus is son of God. He gives us very little information in his letters about the historical Jesus but one thing he does tell us is that Jesus addressed God as his father using the Aramaic *abba* (as in Mark 14:36, though elsewhere the Gospels have the Greek *patēr*), the everyday but respectful form of address of a child to his parent (Romans 8:15; Galatians 4:6). It is misleading to say that Jews did not address God as father but they did it more formally as in '*abēnu, melkenu*', 'our father, our king'. Jesus, speaking in a more domestic way about his Father, was aware of being a son of God in an especially intimate and perhaps experimental way. The point is that in a number of respects Paul says the same of us that he says of Jesus. We too are sons (and daughters) of God. And just as Jesus, as the Son of God, is his Father's heir, so we too are fellow heirs.

For all who are led by the Spirit of God are children of God. For you did not receive a spirit of slavery to fall back into fear, but you have received a spirit of adoption. When we cry 'Abba! Father!' it is that very Spirit bearing witness with our spirit that we are children of God, and if children, then heirs, heirs of God and joint heirs with Christ – if, in fact, we suffer with him so that we may also be glorified with him. (Romans 8:14–17)

As sons and daughters of God, Christian believers are expected to follow Jesus' pattern: they will suffer and will be glorified, and they will receive God's inheritance.

It is the same with death and resurrection. Just as Christ died on the cross, so his followers have died a death, in this case a death to their old lives in baptism.

Do you not know that all of us who have been baptized into Christ Jesus were baptized into his death? Therefore we have been buried with him by baptism into death, so that, just as Christ was raised from the dead by the glory of the Father, so we too might walk in newness of life. (Romans 6:3–4)

So the baptised have died, been buried and raised, like Christ. This is not quite what Paul says. First, no one has literally died at baptism, yet a real, spiritual, albeit metaphorical, death has taken place. The life that was lived before conversion is now a memory. Burial can be envisaged as an entombment under the waters in a baptism by immersion, though Paul does not himself put it that way. What follows, however, is not, according to Paul, resurrection but 'newness of life'. When Paul talks about Jesus' resurrection he uses the past tense, but when he talks about the resurrection of faithful Christians it is always in the future tense.

For if we *have been* united with him in a death like his, we *will* certainly be united with him in a resurrection like his. (Romans 6:5)

For as all die in Adam, so all will be made alive in Christ. But each in his own order: Christ the first fruits, then at his

coming those who belong to Christ. (1 Corinthians 15:22f;
see also 1 Thessalonians 4:13–17)

Christians are destined for resurrection but they have not yet made
it.

This identification of Christ with his followers extends to other
images. In an earlier chapter we saw how we share Christ's righteousness by being faithful to him, just as he was faithful to his
Father. Similarly, as slaves of Christ, we share the status of Christ's
own slavery. This is all part of what Paul says in Philippians about
having the mind of Christ, for what is involved is not just an
intellectual thinking-like Christ – something in the head, as it were
– it is a whole-person identification with Christ. This is a spiritual
identification with Christ from baptism to resurrection and beyond.
Paul's language leaves little space between Christ and his followers.
We are brought so close in this spiritual identification as to be almost
one with him. Christ is not a distant 'other', he is 'the other me'. As
sons and daughters of God with him, he is our brother, but closer
than a brother. This is what Paul means when he says that we live 'in
Christ' and 'in the Lord'. This is not exactly participation in Christ
but identification with him in the way we pattern our lives and in
our final destiny.

Transformed Lives in a Transformed World

Sometimes Paul uses 'in Christ'/'in the Lord' language to contrast
with other ways in which one might live one's life. It contrasts with
how Paul's converts had lived their lives previously, and he characterises this as life in the flesh (Philemon 16) or life in Adam. In
Christ, one's life is transformed at its root, and Paul's Christology is
the basis for this moral and spiritual transformation. But the transformation is a surprising one, full of paradoxes.

The cultural context for Paul's mission to the nations was that of
the Roman Empire, of course. The dominant values of the Empire,
as in all other empires, were power, wealth and pleasure, and the
means for realising them were violence and fear. This was not the
whole story, for Rome was celebrated for bringing Pax Romana to
the world. Civic stability was certainly valued by Paul who was

proud of his Roman citizenship, even though it was the Empire that would execute him in the end. Yet even the Pax Romana was fraudulent in so far as it was designed to preserve the domination of Rome over its conquered nations and, within Rome, to preserve the domination of an elite over the common people. Rome had a seriously unjust political system, though it could be argued that at its best it was more civilised than what lay beyond Rome's frontiers. So, power came through domination, and wealth, as always, was bought through the exploitation of the poor. It was a world of difference: the rulers and the ruled, the rich and the deprived, the exploiters and the exploited. So when Paul announced that there was a new creation, he was announcing the end of this world of injustice and the old gods. The titles of Lord, saviour and god were being taken away from the emperor – who at that time was the young Nero – and given to an executed criminal from Galilee on the eastern edge of the Empire, who, his followers claimed, had been raised from the dead by the God of the Jews.

The old conventional social values were gone and Paul's aim was to subvert the imperial language of power and prestige, just as he subverted the language of slavery. He told the Corinthians that they were fools to the world for the sake of Christ (1 Corinthians 4:10) but that was because 'the message about the cross is foolishness to those who are perishing' (1 Corinthians 1:18). The message of the cross represents the power of God, where God has transformed the world through what the world regards as weakness. Jesus was crucified in weakness but the power of God has given him life (2 Corinthians 13:3). What seemed foolish – the gospel, the message of the cross – is where one now finds wisdom (a theme also found in Matthew 11:25).

> Has not God made foolish the wisdom of the world? For since, in the wisdom of God, the world did not know God through wisdom [and here Paul is probably making a reference to Roman and Greek philosophy], God decided, through the foolishness of our proclamation, to save those who believe. (1 Corinthians 1:20f)

This is why Paul thinks it would be fatuous to be attached to the conventional values of Roman society – and for Roman you can read 'our'. He tells those in Rome not to be conformed to this world but to be transformed, renewed, in order to discover what is the will of God (Romans 12:2). The Philippians are told to work out their salvation in fear and trembling, to become 'blameless and innocent, children of God without blemish in the midst of a crooked and perverse generation, in which you shine like stars in the world' (Philippians 2:15). So our inner natures are being renewed each day (2 Corinthians 4:16).

When Paul says that we must always carry the death of Jesus in our bodies (2 Corinthians 4:10), he is presumably referring to that pattern of life that led Christ to be crushed by Rome: a life of submission rather than assertiveness. Weakness and foolishness in the world may bring suffering and affliction but, in a world turned on its head, this leads to power, wisdom, consolation and life (2 Corinthians 1:3–7). There are signs that living 'in Christ' ultimately belongs in the future, for Paul says that living in the body keeps us away from Christ, where we live by faith and not by sight (2 Corinthians 5:6). Paul looks towards his own resurrection but for that he has to be Christlike in suffering and death. He counts all things in this world as dross because ultimately his citizenship is in heaven, not with Rome (Philippians 3:7–21). Yet at the same time the future in some sense is now. Now is the day of salvation, a theme Paul got from Isaiah (2 Corinthians 6:2 quoting Isaiah 49:8). So everything must be done in the Lord: living, dying, suffering, rejoicing, eating, celebrating (Romans 14:5–9), for he is the one and only foundation of this new world (1 Corinthians 3:11).

The Face of God

We have now seen, by looking at his 'in Christ' language, that Paul sees Christ as the agent of God. To call someone an agent is not necessarily claiming a lot. I can buy a policy from an insurance agent but he is not the one with the finance to protect me. Nor is my insurance agent unique, for there are lots of them. Paul, however, is clear that God has only one agent for transforming the world. So in what way does Paul push his Christology further to claim a status for Jesus that will make him more than just an agent?

Paul develops his thinking about Jesus in a number of stages. First, God has chosen Jesus to be his sole *agent* through whom he now acts in our world. Jesus is then shown to be a *model* whose pattern of life is to be emulated. Because Jesus is a man with a particular historical and social significance but who also presents God to us in a concrete, physical way, Paul urges personal *devotion* to him. Finally, Paul regards Jesus as an object of *worship* to whom prayer should be directed. Paul did not initiate any of this; he discovered it in the church into which he was received, perhaps as early as AD 32 and certainly not long after.

Let us approach this last aspect of Paul's Christology by looking again at 2 Corinthians 3;4—4:6. Here Paul begins by claiming that God has made Jesus a minister of a new covenant, a covenant of the spirit that gives life, not like the old covenant of the letter on tablets of stone – echoing Jeremiah's famous prophecy about a new spiritual covenant (31:31–34). Paul recalls Moses, coming down from the mountain where he had met with God, carrying the stone tablets, with his face shining with a divine radiance from being in the presence of God (Exodus 34:29–35). The Israelites were dazzled by the reflection of God's glory in Moses' face and covered his face with a veil. Paul's version suggests that Moses covered his own face so that the Israelites would not see that the glory of that covenant was already beginning to fade. He says that a veil still lies over their minds when they read the old covenant and the veil can only be removed by turning to Christ. Paul does not here show any of that sympathy for Jewish religion that you see in parts of Romans 9—11. Nonetheless, 'all of us, with unveiled faces' see the glory of the Lord directly and, like Moses, are being transformed into the divine image by that glory. Where is it that *we* see the glory of God? In the face of Jesus Christ, who is the image of God. What Paul actually says is that God gives us 'the light of the knowledge of the glory of God in the face of Jesus Christ' (2 Corinthians 4:6). Paul three times has to qualify his idea that we see the unseeable God. We do not exactly see God, but the *glory* of God; or rather we have the *knowledge* of the glory of God; or better we see the *light* of the knowledge of the glory of God. Nonetheless, despite these qualifications, his basic idea is that when we look on the face of this man we see God, or as much of God as we can see in this lifetime. This is what the incarnation is all about: the idea that in some respect, God and Jesus are to be identified. This verse is the central point of Paul's theology because so much else hangs on it. If we couple it with what we have just said about each Christian having a spiritual identification with Christ, we can see that Paul is making a huge claim about the status of each believer. There is a sense, a reduced sense perhaps, that when we look into the face of, not only self-professed Christians, but anyone, we may see God. This is why faces in icons have been so important in the history of Eastern-rite Christianity.

Paul had little interest in defining doctrine about Christ. After all, there is a limit to how far any doctrine can be defined and doctrinal precision is not something that Paul would have found useful at that time. It has to be said that doctrine is not in the first place a product of an intellectual exercise; its roots are in worship. The idea of the incarnation was not thought out in the abstract; it originated in the instinct of those first Christians who addressed their prayers to Jesus and who made him an object of personal devotion and public worship.[2] Because only God is to be worshipped and only God can answer prayer, it was inevitable that the doctrine of the incarnation would be articulated once Christians like Paul had reflected on the church's practice of prayer. Otherwise one is left with idolatry, treating a creature as though he were a god. Paul says Jesus was born of a woman, born under the law, but he also speaks of Jesus being in the form of God, not hanging on to equality with God but giving up his status to become human and a slave, subject to death. This self-emptying is reversed, however, when God exalts Jesus, has every creature bend the knee and confess that Jesus Christ is Lord (Philippians 2:5–11). Lord (kurios) is a title that could be given to any master, but at the other end of the social scale it was one of the emperor's own titles. Even more importantly, it was the title given to God in the Greek Old Testament translating the mysterious name that God had given to Moses from the burning bush (Exodus 3:14). In calling Jesus 'Lord' exclusively, the emperor was being stripped of the honour he could have expected from his Christian subjects, for Jesus has taken on the supreme lordship of God. The

---

2   For a full discussion of the early church's devotional practices see Larry W. Hurtado, *Lord Jesus Christ: Devotion to Jesus in Earliest Christianity* (Grand Rapids, MI: Eerdmans, 2003). Hurtado argues that Paul inherited an already formed high Christology rather than created one.

author of Colossians, again using an early Christian hymn, calls Jesus 'the image of the invisible God' (echoing 2 Corinthians 4:6), and places him at the centre of the cosmos: everything is created in him, through him and for him – 'for in him all the fullness of God was pleased to dwell' (Colossians 1:15–20). Again in Colossians, 'in him the whole fullness of deity dwells bodily' (Colossians 2:9). This resolves any doubt there might be about the divine status of Jesus in Pauline thinking.

But Paul had to tread a fine line. To stop this becoming one-sided and docetic, Paul – even though he had developed the notion of spiritual identification between humanity and Jesus – had to develop a language of difference for distinguishing God the creator from Jesus of Nazareth. To do this Paul consistently refers to God (*theos*) as Father (as does Jesus in the Gospels), thus clearing the way for Jesus to be called Son. The other titles Paul gives to Jesus, as we have seen, are Christ and that singularly divine title Lord (*kurios*). However, as a good Jew, Paul was immovably monotheist. There cannot be two Gods. But two *somethings* have to be distinguished in the one God. There is the Father and there is the Son, Christ, Lord. Paul brought these together in a Christian confession of faith in 1 Corinthians 8:6, which looks like his attempt to rewrite the Jewish *Shema* for the Christian church. Twice each day a Jew will recite lines that include Deuteronomy 6:4f: 'Hear, O Israel: the Lord our God is one Lord, and you shall love the Lord your God with all your heart and with all your soul and with all your might.' In Paul's adaptation this becomes: 'For us [Christians] there is one God the Father, from whom are all things and for whom we exist; and one Lord, Jesus Christ, through whom are all things and through whom we exist.'

Paul has kept the words Lord and God from Deuteronomy and he has kept oneness. But he has made a distinction between one God and one Lord, between God the Father and the Lord Jesus Christ. All created things come *from* God the Father and *through* the Lord Jesus Christ. We exist *for* the Father and *through* the Lord.[3] Not too much should be read into the meaning of the prepositions

---

3 See Gordon D. Fee, *Pauline Christology: An Exegetical-Theological Study* (Peabody, MA: Hendrickson, 2007), pp. 89–94.

because the important point is Paul's attempt to develop and clarify a language of identity and difference within a tradition of monotheism, producing a kind of binitarianism. Add into that the language for the Spirit and we have a trinity, not yet fully developed but firmly established and finding expression in 2 Corinthians 13:13: 'The grace of the Lord Jesus Christ, the love of God, and the communion of the Holy Spirit be with all of you.'

It was Jesus, God-incarnate, Christ/Messiah, Son and Lord, who had died on the cross and had been raised to life, who had appeared to Paul, who had transformed Paul's life, and who is the foundation for Paul's account of that pattern that should frame the lives of all Christians.

Index

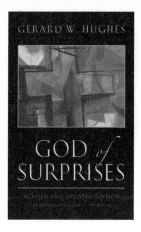

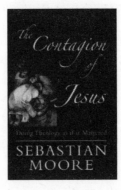